HEARTH & HOME

A rocker washing machine of 1862 in the Tickenhill Collection, founded at Bewdley by the late Mr. and Mrs. J. F. Parker.

HEARTH & HOME
A SHORT HISTORY OF DOMESTIC EQUIPMENT

Sheena Brooke
Illustrated by Shirley Tourret

Mills & Boon Limited, London
in conjunction with The Du Pont Company (UK) Ltd

First published 1973 by Mills & Boon Limited,
17–19 Foley Street, London W1A 1DR

ISBN 0 263.05296.6

Made and printed in Great Britain by
Morrison and Gibb Ltd, London and Edinburgh

Contents

Acknowledgements

My grateful thanks to the following companies and organisations without whose help the writing of this book would have been impossible. I am only sorry that there is not room to list everybody who gave me leads and help with my research.

Alcan Booth Sheet Ltd
Allied English Potteries Ltd
Belling & Co Ltd
Birds Eye Foods Ltd
Bissell Appliances Ltd
The British Brush Manufacturers Research Association
British Domestic Appliances Ltd
Briton Chadwick
Bulpitt & Sons Ltd
Cutlery & Allied Trades Research Association
The Dishwasher Development Council
Domestic Refrigeration Development Committee
The Electricity Council
Electrolux Ltd
Fisher Bendix Ltd
Formica Ltd
Frigidaire Division of General Motors

The Gas Council
The Glass Manufacturers' Federation
Goblin (BVC) Ltd
Hamilton & Co (London) Ltd
Hoover Ltd
Jobling Ltd
Johnson Wax Ltd
Lever Brothers Ltd
Prestige Ltd
Procter & Gamble Ltd
Radiation Ltd
Spode China
Tower Housewares Ltd
Tricity
Unilever
The Wedgwood Group
The Women's Advisory Council on Solid Fuel
The Worcester Royal Porcelain Co Ltd

S.B.

Introduction

In this frenetic age when the average housewife has to be a quick-change artist, coping with the many different rôles within the home from cook to hostess, from housekeeper to gardener and handyman, as well as being a mother, probably a wage-earner, and an attentive wife, it is essential that the equipment she works with is designed for efficiency and easy care.

This book attempts in a small way to show the history and development of some of the major domestic equipment from early days, when labour was plentiful, to today when help in the home is man-made in the form of efficient and effective appliances and surface finishes. Without these man-made aids a woman would be hard pressed to run her home singlehanded.

To give you some idea of the change that has taken place, let us imagine a day in the life of a low-paid office worker's family (who are unable to afford a maid) of, say, a hundred years ago. Let us call them Hill.

Before Mrs. Hill could prepare breakfast she would have to get up heat in the kitchen range, this contraption being the most universal means of cooking and heating water. To do this she would need to riddle out the ashes, causing dust to settle on most of the kitchen furniture, and either relight or stoke up the fire before she could even heat a pot. The range would also need daily black-leading to keep it clean—all hard and very dirty work. Today she would pop downstairs in a dainty housecoat and flick a switch to prepare breakfast for her family.

Most of Mrs. Hill's time and energy would be taken up keeping her small home clean and in good repair. There would be few, if any, easy-care surfaces and so each day the house would need attention. Fires would have to be cleaned out and laid. Floors would require sweeping or mopping over, and rugs and mats would have to be taken outside for shaking or beating by hand. Any wooden floors would need regular scouring with fine sand or fuller's earth to preserve the colour. After the dust had settled Mrs. Hill would polish the furniture, using a home-made polish of beeswax, or a mixture of linseed oil, turpentine, vinegar and probably methylated spirit.

As you can imagine, most of Mrs. Hill's morning would be devoted to just cleaning the downstairs rooms. Today the housewife can easily clean her whole house in a morning with the aid of a carpet sweeper or vacuum cleaner. Her furniture would only require a quick wipe over, using one of the many varieties of polish, each tailored for a specific surface, which both clean and give a long-lasting shine with the minimum of rubbing.

In earlier times, clearing up after the mid-day meal would be a laborious business. Greasy dishes would need particular attention as there were no synthetic detergents to help dissolve the fat. Pots and pans would require harsh scouring both inside and out to keep the iron surfaces clean and free from rust.

After the general washing up, the wooden surfaces in the kitchen would need hard scrubbing, as wood in those days was usually untreated. Today there are a large number of modern finishing materials available for the surface coating and sealing of wood both for floors and furniture. These lacquers, such as polyurethane and polyester, give a finish which is hard and glossy, resistant to heat and abrasion. The lacquered surfaces are easily cared for and only need a wipe over with a damp cloth to clean.

During the afternoon Mrs. Hill might continue to clean her house or clean her silver, brass, copper, and pewter ware. She would probably have her own special recipes for metal polishes, or for brass she might use charcoal or bonefire ash. Interestingly, charcoal is still used today in the Royal Mews to clean brass that is fitted to leather as it doesn't discolour the leather. Regular weekly polishing sessions would be needed to keep Mrs. Hill's metals bright. Today modern long-term polishes for all the household metals are available, which will clean them and give a protection against tarnish for several weeks—the duration depending of course on how often the metals are used and where you live.

As you delve into this book you will find more examples of how modern technology has provided the housewife with appliances and easy-care products that help to take the hard labour and time out of just about every chore; even ironing, so time-consuming, has been reduced by the introduction of so many non-iron fabrics both for household linen and personal clothing, and by improvements in the design of the iron itself.

An important point to remember is that without the development of the small electric motor during the latter part of the 19th century, it would have been difficult, if not impossible, to produce the sophisticated domestic appliances we all take for granted today.

1 Cooking

WHAT THEY ATE

Primitive man lived from hand to mouth on a simple diet of wild fruits, nuts and any small animals he could catch with patience and cunning.

Only when he discovered fire was he able to supplement his diet with cereals (wild grass seeds) and meat, because his digestive system could only cope with these additional foods when they were softened and tenderised by cooking.

Man's first attempt at cooking was probably roasting small rodents beside or on his fire. His first effort at boiling was perhaps by scraping out a small hole near the fire, lining it with animal skins, filling it with cold water and then putting in the meat or grain to be cooked, and finally dropping in hot stones from his fire until the water was hot enough to cook the food. The first principles of immersion heating!

The art of cooking took an important step forward during Neolithic times when our ancestors learnt to domesticate animals and to grow cereals, and to make simple earthenware pots.

Both the Romans and the Greeks had sophisticated ideas on the art of cooking and on table manners. The Romans introduced these to Britain. When they left, the country was conquered by the savage Angles and Saxons, who had never known and cared little for these refinements. Gradually the Anglo-Saxons settled down and became more civilised, and the Normans added new ideas about food and cookery, but still without regaining the heights of Roman luxury.

Family dinner, probably before 1300.
By permission of the Radio Times
Hulton Picture Library.

MEDIEVAL FOOD

A brief look at the kind of food and dishes eaten by our ancestors may help you understand why the shape of the pot and pan didn't change much until the introduction of the kitchen range in the early 19th century.

Britain was economically and socially divided into the wealthy landowners and merchants and the labourers who worked for them.

Food was home grown, without much agricultural know how, and was subject to the whims of the climate—there might be three years of good harvests and then a year when crops were ruined by storms, which meant short rations for all, and probably famine conditions for the poor.

In Anglo-Saxon times, the contrast between the quality and the quantity of the food eaten by the landowner and the labourer wasn't outstandingly great. It generally consisted of pottage, a type of thick stew-like soup made of oatmeal or a mixture of vegetables, such as cabbage, turnips, onions, leeks or beans, and maybe a piece of pork. The richer households might have made their pottage of finely ground meat. This was eaten with rough brown bread and soft cheese. On high days and holidays there was the welcome addition of small game, pig, fowl or fish. All was washed down with ale.

The distinction between landowner and labourer was much greater during the Middle Ages. The labourer was still eating dark rye bread with pottage and soft cheese and the occasional piece of pork or ham, while the Lord of the Manor, his family, friends, servants and retainers might eat roasted venison (considered a luxury), roasted beef and mutton, roasted pigs, various thick pottages, meat pies, accompanied by rich sauces. There was usually a second course of fish, roasted pheasant, roasted herons, poultry, fruit pies or tarts; washed down with ale for the servants and with wine for the lord, his family and guests. It was the custom for the whole household and servants to eat together in the Great Hall.

A CHANGE IN EATING HABITS

The 16th century fare of the working classes still consisted of vegetable pottage, with beef or pork once a week, as well as home-grown fruits, jam sweetened with honey, cheese, coarse bread, and ale.

In the manor house the family was now less inclined to take the main meal of the day in the Great Hall; the privacy of a small room or chamber—ultimately to become the dining-room—might be preferred. By this time the Great Hall was used mainly for entertaining, when grand feasts were called for.

The food was probably more delicately spiced, and there were sweet dishes, such as custards. These, by the way, were baked in front of the open fire.

The 17th and 18th centuries saw a revolution in farming, with the provision of winter food for animals, and an improvement in stock-breeding by Robert Bakewell and the Brothers Collings. Previous to this most stock animals, except those used for breeding, were slaughtered in the autumn as no provision was made for fodder to keep the animals through the winter. The meat was heavily salted so that it would keep, and cannot have made a very interesting diet.

However, the basic diet of the 17th century working man followed the pattern of previous centuries—pottage, bread, cheese with the occasional luxury of meat when he could afford it and fish when he could catch it.

There was increasing prosperity amongst the merchants or middle classes with the growing trade abroad, particularly with the East. Chocolate, coffee and tea were now added to their menu. Potatoes were no longer a novelty, and fresh meat, due to improved farming methods, was available throughout the year at a price. Meals were now taken in the dining-room, and the food, though still extravagant by our standards, was not so over-whelming.

The land enclosures towards the end of the 18th century brought extremes of poverty and hunger to the working people, particularly the villagers. Their diet tended to consist of thin vegetable soup, bread and anything else they could scrounge.

19th century Victorian England brought great wealth to the industrialists and nothing but grinding labour and starvation to the majority of workers. Their main meal was probably thin potato soup with bread, and some very weak tea or ale for the fortunate or just hot water for the unlucky.

KITCHENWARE

From this very brief history of our ancestors' eating habits you will see that the poor required little more than a couple of pots in which to cook their meagre food over an open fire.

The cooking in cottages and farmhouses from medieval times until the 17th century was undertaken in the living room; while in large manor houses and castles the kitchen was a separate room, usually a large lean-to away from the main part of the house in case of fire, which was quite a hazard when you think of the combination of open fires, hot fat from roasting meat and the timber-framed buildings.

Until the kitchen range was introduced in the early 19th century all cooking, with the exception of baking, was done over an open fire (see chapter 2). This meant that pots were designed to sit on or hang over the fire, and pans were placed at the edge of, or on, the fire, or held over the flames by long handles. So the designs and shapes haven't really changed for some 2,000 years.

METHODS OF COOKING

The principal methods of cooking, until the invention of the range, were roasting in front of the open fire, broiling over the fire, boiling or stewing, and baking in an oven which was quite separate from the open hearth.

Baking was generally undertaken on a specific day, as the oven had to be specially prepared and heated.

POT FOR BOILING OR STEWING

Can you imagine cooking over an open fire? None of today's elegant, light-weight pans would be practical. They would quickly blacken, and be in danger of overbalancing with the movement of the fire. But this was how our ancestors cooked.

Cooking equipment had to be tough, versatile and able to balance on a log fire as well as stand on the ground beside the fire.

The round-based iron cauldron with three short stocky legs was found to be the most practical. This basic, sturdy shape changed hardly at all until the introduction of the cooking range. The only change came in the attachments for moving the cauldrons on and off the fire.

The cauldron was used for stewing or boiling meat, making thick stews or pottages; and, no doubt, for heating water for the very occasional laundry day or bath.

When the hearth was moved to one side of the room, cauldrons and pots could now be hung over the fire from an iron rod or pot-hook let into the brickwork of the chimney piece. Some of these rods were adjustable and known as ratchets, which meant the pots could be lowered or raised as the cooking required. It must have made life more comfortable for the cook, since he could then adjust the temperature of the mixture in the pot by raising or lowering the pot on the ratchet rather than having to struggle to move a boiling cauldron off an open fire. So, instead of regulating the heat as we do today by turning up or down the gas or electricity, the pot was moved up or down as required on the ratchet.

CHIMNEY CRANE

The next improvement was the chimney crane which began to appear in the 17th century. This consisted of a hinged, horizontal bar fixed to the side of the fireplace, onto which was forged a hanging piece with a hook to hold cauldrons and pots.

The crane allowed pots to be moved up and down over the fire, and it could also swing away from or back over the hearth, rather like a gate. A crane could be extremely elaborate or very simple, depending on whether it was to be used in a great house or a humble cottage.

SKILLETS AND SAUCEPANS

For cooking small quantities of food an iron skillet was used. A skillet resembled the saucepan used today. It had a longer iron handle to make it more manageable over the hot open fire, and three short legs, like the cauldron, for balance on the fire.

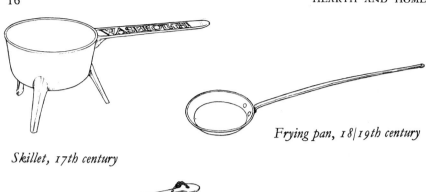

Frying pan, 18/19th century

Skillet, 17th century

Toaster, 18/19th century

Iron pot, 18/19th century

Cauldron, 18/19th century

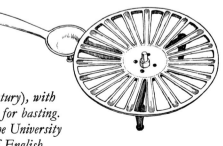

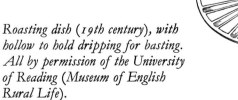

Roasting dish (19th century), with hollow to hold dripping for basting. All by permission of the University of Reading (Museum of English Rural Life).

A saucepan was any kind of small, deep-sided pan with a handle, used for making sauces. It might be made of iron, bronze or copper. Sauces tended to be milk-based and required a gentle heat, so the saucepan would be set on a trivet or hob (see below) before the fire, or directly at the edge of the hearth with hot ashes heaped round and underneath it.

FRYING PANS

There were two main types of frying pans for use on an open hearth. One was a heavy iron pan which was very similar in shape to the kind used today, except that it had a very long metal handle to allow the user to stand well away from the heat of the fire and the spluttering fat.

The other kind had a half-hoop handle with a ring for hanging from a pot-hook or ratchet.

At the Cambridge and County Folk Museum there is a long-handled 18th century iron frying pan with its own frame which hung from the pot-hook, so the pan could be held directly over the fire for searing the meat and then placed in the frame hanging over the fire for more gentle cooking.

GRILLERS

The grill or gridiron was used for searing and cooking small pieces of meat, such as chops or steak, by placing the meat on the gridiron over the direct heat of the open fire.

The simplest form was a row of iron bars set into a frame with a very long handle, allowing the cook to stand well clear of the spitting fat. It looked rather like the grill used today, without the pan. A more elaborate gridiron sometimes had a hinged upper frame, so that the meat was securely held between two frames.

TRIVETS AND HOBS

The cook using an open hearth was at the mercy of the whims of the fire. He had little control over its heat. The only way he could regulate the heat was to move the pot or pan itself over or away from the fire as the cooking proceeded. The chimney crane, pot hook or ratchet helped the cook to govern the speed of cooking by allowing a certain movement of the pot up or down, away or over the fire.

Trivet and hobs were small metal stands used round the edge of the hearth for holding saucepans, warming plates, and for keeping food hot. The trivet had three legs and the hob had four.

Chimney cranes, pot-hooks, ratchets, trivets and hobs were all considered labour-saving devices. They meant that the food could, within reason, be left to look after itself, allowing the cook or kitchen assistants to get on with other work.

SPITS FOR ROASTING

Roasting is possibly the earliest form of cooking known to man. Our ancestors would thread small birds, animals or fish onto wooden skewers and set them before the fire to roast.

During the lifetime of the open hearth this method of cooking didn't change. But the skewers and spits developed from wood or simple iron rods turned by hand to sophisticated clockwork bottle jacks which had a winding mechanism.

The iron age saw the development of iron spits hung between iron fire-dogs or andirons over a bed of hot ashes. The fire-dogs' main use was to prevent large logs rolling off the hearth. They could be as simple or elaborate as the household could afford, and the blacksmith fashion. On the elaborate ones there might be three levels of brackets to hold the spits, as well as various hooks for pots and perhaps a small iron basket set on top of each fire-dog, on which dishes or pots could be warmed before the fire.

TYPES OF SPITS

There were probably as many designs of spits as there were blacksmiths to make them. The three main types, of which there were many variations, were:

a *straight spit* onto which poultry and game could be slipped;

a *pronged spit* which was for holding large joints of meat which otherwise would have been spoilt by piercing. There were either one or two prongs. The two-pronged style could be moved along the spit to accommodate the size of the joint to be roasted. This design of spit is found on some of today's rotisseries;

Roasting on the spit and other cooking activities. From the Luttrell Psalter, 14th century. By permission of the Radio Times Hulton Picture Library

a *basket or cradle spit* was used for roasting sucking pig and other small animals. The steel bars making the basket were removable to allow the meat to be put inside.

A small pan was placed below the revolving spit to catch the fat or 'dripping', which was used for basting the roasting meat. This dripping was stored in a heavy three legged-pan, called a grease pan.

Turnspit at work, about 1790. Above the fireplace is a spit rack. By permission of the Radio Times Hulton Picture Library.

One of the main uses for this dripping was for making rushlights and candles.

When the spits were not in use they were kept on a spit rack above the fireplace.

TYPES OF SPIT MOVEMENTS

The early spit was turned by hand, usually by some small kitchen boy or scullion. He was known as a turnspit.

During Tudor times some genius thought up the idea of using a dog running on a treadmill to turn the chain and wheel which operated the spit.

By the end of the 18th century the *smoke jack* was in use in Britain, though it had been used on the Continent for some centuries before reaching these islands.

The smoke jack was operated by a large wooden fan which hung in the narrow neck of the chimney. The fan was turned by the rising current of hot air from the fire. The power created drove the various gears and pulleys which turned the spit. The snag was that a large fire was needed to create sufficient hot air to drive the mechanism.

The *Clockwork bottle jack*, introduced in the 19th century, was an improvement on the smoke jack in that it didn't rely on the heat of the fire for movement, and so could be used when a large fire was not possible or necessary.

It contained a clockwork mechanism which, when the jack was wound up with a key, turned it in a clockwise and then in an anticlockwise direction until the meat was cooked. It was a hanging device and so took up less room on the hearth.

The jack could also be placed within a metal screen or 'hastener' in front of the fire. The screen kept the draughts away and reflected heat onto the meat, so hastening the cooking. Any basting was done through a door in the front of the screen.

Not every household boasted a spit. According to Dr. Johnson small joints could be managed by a piece of string, and the larger ones could be cooked at the local tavern!

OVEN PRACTICE

Until the innovation of the kitchen range, ovens were, in general, separate from the open hearth (see page 40).

The majority of the poor had no oven and baked their bread by the open hearth, using a *flat stone* or a *griddle*. This was covered with an earthenware pot or an iron cauldron turned upside down; hot embers or burning peat were then piled round it. Pies and tarts might be taken to the local bakery for cooking.

When there was an oven it usually projected from the wall, as it wasn't practical to build it into the wattle and daub wall of a cottage.

In large houses the bakehouse was usually apart from the main kitchen, and the oven was built into the thickness of the wall.

All these ovens were heated by a fire made of wood mixed with dried faggots lit on the floor of the oven. When the oven was hot enough the ashes were raked out and the floor cleaned.

Bake day, like laundry day, was an event and usually took place once a week or once a fortnight. It had to be planned in advance as, for economy reasons, every atom of oven heat was utilised. Bread, pastries, pies, cakes and custards were cooked in the stored heat, and any residue heat would be used for drying fruit, herbs and the wood for the next week's bake.

The Camp oven appeared on the market in 1782. It was a portable oven and when filled with bread and cakes could be set in the fire. It must have been rather a hot job removing it when the baking was finished.

Turnspit worked by smoke, Italian, 1656. By permission of the Radio Times Hulton Picture Library.

A major development in the closed oven, as we understand it today, came with the invention of the kitchen range in 1780. This was an oven built into the stove; initially it was heated only on the side nearest the fire. So there must have been some lop-sided baking results! It was not until 1840 with the arrival of the Kitchener range (see page 43) that we were set on our way to today's methods of cooking.

SHAPES

The development of the closed Kitchener range brought about a change in shape of cooking ware. It wasn't radical—the base became flat to match the flat surface of the closed stove.

Sizes were reduced as households reduced and also because the closed stove was able to support many more pots and pans than the open hearth. As menus became more elaborate so did the range of pots and pans.

EARLY MATERIALS

The earliest materials for cooking equipment were mainly stone and pottery, then progressing to iron, with the coming of the iron age, and to other metals as they were discovered and worked.

Until the 1750s cooking utensils were mainly of brass, bronze, copper and iron. A lot of hard work and time must have been needed to keep the pots and pans of these eras bright and clean.

A method of *tin-coating* the inside of cast and wrought ironware was introduced during the latter half of the 18th century. This prevented pots from rusting when not in use.

From the beginning of the 19th century pots were finished on the outside with a *black varnish*. Both tin-plating and varnishing would reduce the labour of cleaning. Copper and brass pans still needed scouring and polishing.

Cooking utensils, from Mrs. Beeton's Household Management, *1894. By permission of the Radio Times Hulton Picture Library.*

STOCK-POT.

BAIN-MARIE.

STEW-PAN.

BRAIZING PAN.

BLOCK-TIN SAUCEPAN.

BOILING-POT.

UBLE, OR MILK, SAUCEPAN.

IRON SAUCEPAN, WITH STEAMER.

OMELETTE PAN.

SAUTÉ-PAN.

FRICANDEAU PAN.

PRESERVING PAN AND SPOON.

SALMON KETTLE.

TURBOT KETTLE.

FISH KETTLE.

The end of the 19th century brought an improved finishing process—*vitreous enamelling*. The first application of enamel to sheet iron and steel occurred in Germany around 1850.

The craft of enamelling precious ornaments and jewellery goes back to biblical times, but during the Dark Ages the art of enamelling was lost to Europe. It was rediscovered during the Middle Ages and was a privilege of the rich and used for precious objects, sacred and otherwise.

Vitreous enamel—known as porcelain enamel in America—is glass which is applied to metal by firing. In the heat of the furnace it flows evenly and smoothly over the surface to be covered, and sets with a hard, smooth, durable finish which is clean and cool to the touch.

The enamelling of cheap metals, such as cast iron, came about some 150 years ago with the need to protect the surface of the iron from chemical action. It was used on such objects as clock faces, shop signs, instruments and, of course, kitchen utensils. It gave a better protection than tinplating against the chemical reaction on metal of some foodstuffs.

The real expansion of the use of this labour-saving finish began early in the 20th century and gathered speed with the introduction of labour-saving domestic appliances.

Aluminium was first produced in 1825 by a Dane, H. C. Oerstedt, and in 1852 it cost $545 per pound!—more expensive than gold. It became an economic proposition in 1886 when Charles Martin Hall, a graduate of Oberlin College, Ohio, discovered how to produce it by an electrolytic process. At about the same time a Frenchman, Paul L. T. Heroult of Paris, made the same discovery. In 1888 a German chemist, Karl Joseph Bayer, issued a patent for an improved process for making aluminium oxide from low-silica content bauxite ores. And so aluminium was launched as an economically commercial metal.

Aluminium was first used for domestic holloware around the latter part of the 19th century. It was the ideal material for this purpose as manufacturers found that it was easy to work and form and required relatively little machinery to produce holloware.

20th CENTURY MATERIALS AND FINISHES

Since the beginning of the 20th century there has been a considerable development in the number of materials and finishes available for cooking ware. The housewife, since the end of the Second World War, has put easy cleaning and dual-purpose space-savers, such as oven-to-table ware, at the top of her requirements for good holloware. As a result two major developments have occurred—the increasing use of and demand for non-stick finishes (see pp. 30–31) for all types of holloware, and the increasing fashion for oven-to-table ware both ovenproof and flame-proof.

The following are some of the main materials and finishes in use today:

ALUMINIUM

Aluminium is lightweight, which makes it easy to handle. It is an excellent conductor of heat, in that it spreads heat evenly and quickly. It doesn't discolour food or flavour it, and has a good resistance to fatty acids.

The finishes and coatings applied to aluminium holloware were traditionally plain until the mid-1960s, although colour had been introduced to the lids by an anodising treatment. In this an oxide film is given to the surface of the metal and then this layer can be dyed.

The most revolutionary finish has been the development of non-stick cookware. The non-stick coatings are based on a plastic, polytetrafluorethylene (PTFE). The most recent technique, introduced into Britain in 1967 as 'Teflon' non-stick finish, involved the application of two different layers of coating. A further improvement has been the special treatment known as 'hard base', which results in a scratch-resistant non-stick coating (see page 31).

Since the mid-1960s the exterior decoration of aluminium cooking utensils has undergone exciting changes with the introduction of highly coloured porcelain enamelled and polyamide finishes, and even more recently with the development of gay screen-printed patterns.

Several ranges of coloured porcelain-enamelled aluminium pans with 'Teflon' non-stick interiors have been launched. The porcelain-enamel is colourful and easy to maintain, with the advantages of aluminium's quick and even heat distribution. However, rough treatment should be avoided as it may cause scratching and chipping of the porcelain-enamel.

STAINLESS STEEL

This is a hard, tough, highly durable metal, which is not easily stained and is convenient to keep clean. However, it does not conduct heat very well. Stainless steel pans usually have an aluminium or copper base to distribute heat evenly. This type of cookware tends to cost more than aluminium.

Stainless steel was developed in 1910 but it didn't arrive in the kitchen for cookware until the late 1920s and early 1930s. By this time enamelled cookware was well established, and, moreover, inexpensive; so stainless steel didn't really establish itself in the domestic market until the 1950s.

CAST IRON

Cast-iron pots and pans are excellent for long, slow cooking. They are durable and have an even heat spread, but are heavy and tend to rust if not oiled after use. They are rarely found in the home today without some form of finish, the main one being vitreous enamel (see page 26). Cast iron is porous, which makes it an ideal metal for enamelling as it holds the enamel fast.

Vitreous enamelled cast-iron ware is both flameproof and ovenproof and the range includes stew pans, casseroles, terrines, saucepans, gratin dishes, skillets and frying pans.

ENAMELLED STEEL

This material is a lighter and cheaper substitute for cast iron. For the most efficient use it should have a ground base for use on hotplates. It is used for both pots and pans and oven-to-table ware.

COPPER

Copper cookware is a good conductor of heat. It requires to be lined with tin, tin nickel or stainless steel, and must be relined when the lining shows any sign of wear. This is because copper is liable to become coated with verdigris, a poisonous substance, on exposure to a moist atmosphere or on contact with acetic acid.

STONEWARE (also see page 80)

Stoneware is ovenproof and sometimes flameproof and its main use is for oven-to-table ware.

BOROSILICATE GLASS

This is a glass with a high thermal shock resistance, that is, it will resist considerable heat. It is widely used for oven-to-table ware.

It was first manufactured in Britain in 1921, although it had been used in America for some years, and it is best known to us as 'Pyrex'. One of the main ingredients is borax, which reduces the rate of heat expansion.

CERAMIC GLASS

Cookware made from this tempered glass is ovenproof and flameproof, and highly resistant to changes of temperature. It can be used straight from the home freezer and put on a naked flame, under a grill or in an oven without damage.

It is made from pyroceram, a material developed for the nose cones of guided missiles. It was introduced to this country from America in the early 1960s.

PORCELAIN (also see page 78)

This material, designed for oven-to-table ware, is ovenproof and usually flameproof. It is translucent, hard-wearing and heat resistant. Traditionally French, it is made in Britain by the Worcester Royal Porcelain Company.

NON-STICK FINISHES

The great revolution in kitchen equipment has been the development of polytetrafluoroethylene (PTFE) coated non-stick cookware. PTFE, the basis for 'Teflon' non-stick finish, has some remarkable properties. It is unaffected by heat or cold over a very wide range of temperatures, and is very slippery. This last characteristic is the one which makes it so useful in the kitchen, as it can be quickly and easily cleaned.

DISCOVERY

PTFE was discovered in 1938 by Dr. Roy Plunkett of the Du Pont Company, USA, while he was working on refrigerants. However, the idea of using it for cooking utensils didn't occur until the mid-1950s, with the large scale production of domestic non-stick ware in America in 1962.

MANUFACTURE

The application of 'Teflon*' coating is a highly sophisticated operation which results in a non-stick finish for cookware which will not flake or peel.

The coating consists of two layers of different composition. The first layer contains materials which guarantee the permanent adhesion of the non-stick material to the metal of the cookware. Over this first layer goes the top coat which has maximum non-stick properties and also contains the pigments that give the coating its colour. Each coating is sprayed onto the article to be covered and then it is baked in at a temperature up to 400° C (190° F.)

---

* 'Teflon' is the Du Pont Company's trademark for PTFE. Du Pont do not make cookware, they supply makers of pots and pans with 'Teflon' which is applied under licence.

To guarantee quality Du Pont award their quality seal only to manufacturers who regularly submit samples of their coated ware to the testing laboratory.

The quality control tests check the thickness of the coating, the adhesion of the coating to the metal and its resistance to scratching and abrasion. The surface is inspected for any marks or irregularities which could affect the performance of the pot or pan.

RECENT DEVELOPMENT

A recent development has been *scratch resistant* non-stick coating which allows the use of metal kitchen utensils without damage to the coating.

The metal underneath the coating is covered with a layer of extremely hard micro-particles which form peaks and valleys. The non-stick finish is then applied between and over these peaks. These peaks and valleys are not visible to the naked eye, but they cause the equipment used for cooking such as metal spoons, forks and spatulas, to 'bounce' off them and so prevent deep scratching of the surface. Any scratching which might occur will be very slight and will remain superficial.

IN THE HOME

In 1967 'Teflon' non-stick finish was introduced to Britain, where it is available on stew pans, casseroles, saucepans, frying pans and a variety of bakeware, as well as on egg poachers and slicers, and on rolling pins.

It has two important advantages:

Easy cleaning—no scraping or scouring, and soaking is rarely necessary. A quick wash in hot water with a detergent, followed by a rinse, is all that is needed. A pan coated with, say white sauce or custard can be quickly washed out after making the sauce or custard and used again immediately, so saving the housewife a pile of pans to wash up at the end of preparing a meal.

Fatless cooking—foods can be cooked without fat, an important point for anyone on a fat-free diet. A moderate temperature is recommended for frying without fat.

Fat *can* be used for frying but you probably won't require as much fat as with a traditional pan.

Bakeware—cake tins with non-stick surfaces need not be lined. Bun tins become very easy to clean, and the advantages of non-stick rolling pins are obvious.

*Illustrations on this and the opposite
page by permission of the University
of Reading (Museum of Rural Life).*

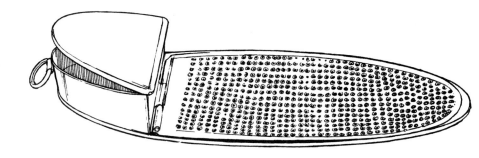

Nutmeg grater, 19/20th century.

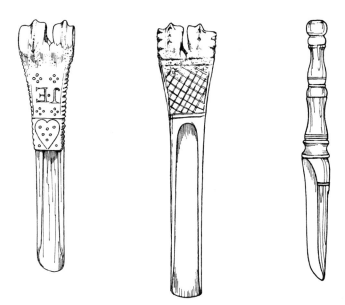

*Apple corers in use from 17th
century. First two are made from
bone.*

SOME OTHER KITCHEN WARE

Kitchen tools, such as long-handled ladles and mixing spoons, skimmers for soup, and knives for chopping and cutting meat, didn't change much over the centuries. The basic shapes are still used today but the tools are smaller and more manageable and lighter.

There were many different kinds of *toasters*. In fact, until the advent of the grill, any two or three pronged implement was used for toasting. But our ancestors, like ourselves, looked for ways and means of saving time and labour, so they devised a freestanding toaster—a tripod with a pronged upright to hold the toast. An elaborate model might have a rim on which a small dripping basin could be set, so the toaster could also be used for roasting small birds or pieces of meat.

On some models the pronged attachment could be raised or lowered to catch the heat of the fire, or could be turned so that the bread didn't have to be turned round. Some trivets had a toasting fork attachment.

Electric freestanding toasters have been in use since the 1920s, but the early models were not very reliable or safe. Today safety is a major consideration and often influences the design of the appliance. Two convenient features on modern toasters are the shade selection control which allows the user to choose the shade of toast preferred; and the pop up feature which occurs when the bread is correctly toasted.

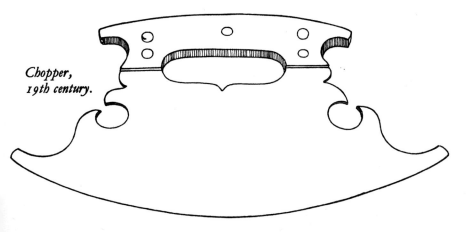

Chopper,
19th century.

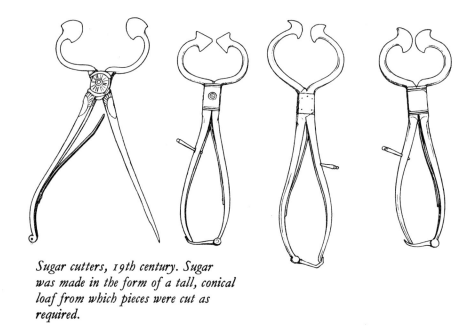

*Sugar cutters, 19th century. Sugar
was made in the form of a tall, conical
loaf from which pieces were cut as
required.*

The *Salamander* was a very simple but ingenious device used in the past to
brown food such as a dish of potatoes or pastry. Remember there were no
grills to pop food under for browning. A Salamander was a block of
metal with a long handle which was heated in the fire until red hot and
then held over the dish to be browned.

Wafering irons were used for baking a type of rich, sweet biscuit and were
in use until the early 19th century. In pre-Reformation times these irons
had been used for preparing wafer bread for ecclesiastical purposes.

The wafering irons looked like a pair of tongs with two flat discs which
were decorated on the inner sides. The irons were heated in the fire, the
batter mixture was poured onto a disc and the discs were closed. The
cooked biscuit was marked with the pattern on the discs.

Today we use very similar utensils for preparing waffles and wafers. The
main development is that this modern cookware is coated inside with
non-stick, easy-to-clean Teflon finish.

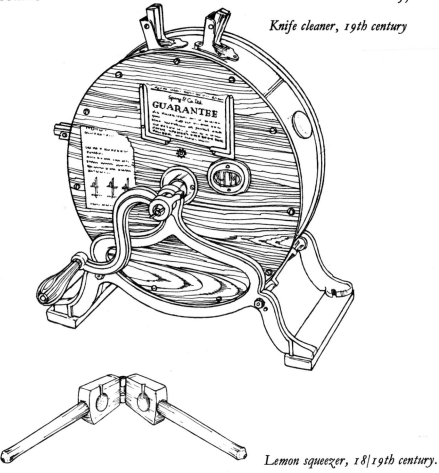

Knife cleaner, 19th century

Lemon squeezer, 18/19th century.

Pastry case for mince pies, 19th century.

All by permission of the University of Reading (Museum of English Rural Life).

Tea and coffee were not introduced into this country until the late 17th century and then were only drinks for the wealthy; hot water is not a very comforting drink, so our ancestors, children included, used to drink 'mulled' or warmed beer and ale. This was heated in a cone or boot shaped vessel, known as a *beer warmer*, which was a very practical shape for pushing into the hot embers of the fire for heating. Beer warmers were usually made of tinned copper, although some were of iron.

A *food chopping machine* was in use in the later 19th and early 20th century for chopping vegetables and the ingredients for mincemeat. The food to be chopped was put in a wooden based drum, and when the handle was turned the drum revolved and the chopping knife moved up and down. There are examples of this machine in the Cambridge and County Folk Museum, Cambridge, and the Welsh Folk Museum, Cardiff.

The *kettle* was originally a large open pan used for boiling; hence the phrase 'a pretty kettle of fish'. There is little information about the development of the early kettle to the heavy black cast-iron ones seen in most folk museums. These hung from a ratchet over the open hearth and were the main hot water supply.

The vogue for tea-drinking, no doubt, helped to bring about a variety of sizes and metals, such as copper and brass.

The first electric kettle was seen at the Chicago World's Fair of 1893. The heating element of the early electric kettle was fixed to the base, which was inefficient, as it was necessary to heat the base of the kettle as well as the water. It was also unreliable, clumsy and no doubt dangerous.

In 1921 the first immersion element for electric kettles was produced. The element sleeve was soldered into the body of the kettle and the bottom was then soldered on. There was no safety device in that there were two separate insulated terminal plugs, so theoretically you could put on the live plug and complete the circuit by holding the neutral terminal in your own hand.

Today there are two main types—the automatic and non-automatic. The automatic kettle switches itself off when the water is boiling. Another refinement is an on/off feature which keeps the water close to boiling if the kettle is left unattended.

Bakeware with the 'Teflon' non-stick finish offers easy release.

Some of the colourful cast-iron cookware available with 'Teflon' non-stick PTFE surfaces. By permission of Waterford Colorcast.

Pressure cookers, with 'Teflon' finish inside for easy cleaning.
By permission of Prestige Ltd.

Pressure cookers, with 'Teflon' finish inside for easy cleaning.
By permission of Prestige Ltd.

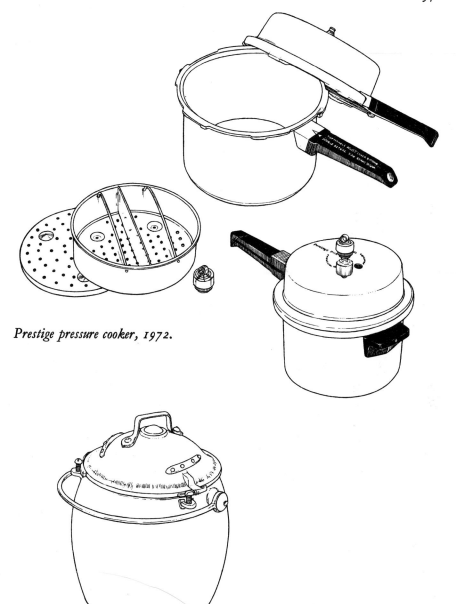

Prestige pressure cooker, 1972.

'Digester' (early pressure cooker) 19th century.

The forerunner of today's *pressure cooker* was Papin's 'Digester', invented in 1681 by Denis Papin the French scientist, to extract gelatine from bones.

It was a heavy cast-iron pot with a tightly fitting lid containing a valve which opened when the steam pressure was too high.

The early models were too heavy and clumsy for domestic use but were being used by restaurants in the late 19th century.

The basis of the pressure cooker is that the high pressure allows liquids to be heated above their normal boiling point. When hot water boils under pressure the temperature rises and cooking takes place more quickly. The fact that the pot is sealed helps to retain the flavour of the food.

Today there are various types of pressure cooker. The latest models have a non-stick PTFE finish for easy cleaning.

Electric food mixers are a post 1939–45 war development in this country. One of the first models was a simple hand-held type which the housewife used with her usual mixing bowl. In 1947 a freestanding table model food mixer was developed. The basic shape of this type of mixer has changed very little, except that the stove-enamelled finish has given way to a light metal pressing and plastic casing, making the whole machine much lighter in weight.

The main types in use today are: the *table model* with such attachments as blender, slicer, shredder, mincer, potato peeler, can opener, coffee grinder, juice extractor. The *hand-held mixer*, available with or without a stand, is useful for creaming fat and sugar, whisking eggs and stirring. *Blenders or liquidisers* are useful for purees, blending soups, fruits and vegetable juices, making breadcrumbs, and mayonnaise—in fact any food which needs to be pulverised or reduced to liquid form.

FURTHER READING

Teflon, Du Pont Information Service, Du Pont Company (United Kingdom) Ltd, 18 Bream's Buildings, Fetter Lane, London, E.C.4.

A Baronial Household in the Thirteenth Century. Margaret Wade Labarge. Eyre & Spottiswoode, 1965.

The English Housewife in the Seventeenth Century. Christina Hole. Chatto & Windus, 1953.

English Home-Life 1500–1800. Christina Hole. Batsford, 1947.

Housekeeping in the Eighteenth Century. Rosamond Bayne-Powell. John Murray, 1956.

Meals Through the Ages. Peter Moss. George G. Harrap & Co. Ltd, 1958.

How Things Developed—Food. Molly Harrison. The Educational Supply Association Ltd, 1955.

The Story of the Kitchen. S. E. Ellacott. Methuen, 1953.

Kitchen and Table. Colin Clair. Abelard Schuman, 1964.

2 From Hearth to Stove

The open hearth, until the 13th century, was generally situated in the centre of the room, or the great hall. The smoke found its own way out through a hole in the roof. A very hit and miss affair when you consider the many draughts which must have blown the smoke anywhere but up through the hole.

The hearth was the cosiest place in the house. Here the cooking was done, and people gathered to warm themselves and gossip. It was the heart of the home.

With the development of the chimney in the 13th century the open hearth was moved to a side wall, where the fire was set into a deep recess below a wide flue. The hearth was still open and still the cooking area, except in large establishments where there was usually a separate kitchen. In these large kitchens there were moreover two or more wall-fireplaces. St. Fagan's Castle kitchen at the Welsh Folk Museum, Cardiff, had two large fireplaces, and the kitchen at Glastonbury Abbey had no less than four.

The fuel was wood or peat until the 15th century, when coal slowly became fashionable in large towns. However, the majority of country folk continued to use wood or peat until the 19th century, as it was the cheapest form of fuel. The labourer was allowed to take all the dead wood that he could manage from the hedgerows, 'by hook or by crook'—using his shepherd's crook or his weeding hook. He was not allowed to cut wood.

By the latter part of the 16th century coal was being used more frequently in town homes. Its use brought about the development of the raised fireplace with the iron fire basket, and the cooking range.

THE SOLID FUEL RANGE

Until the 18th century most cookery was arranged for open hearth fires. Now with the introduction of the range, it was possible to bake, braise, roast, stew and boil on one appliance.

The change from open-hearth cooking to the stove came gradually, starting with an invention by Hornbuckle in 1769. This was an iron oven which could be placed behind an open fire-grate, with passages round the oven to carry the heat. In 1783, Langmead patented an oven which could be set at one side of an open fire-grate, with a boiler for hot water on the other side. It is doubtful if these developments were very efficient, but they were a step in the right direction.

Towards the end of the 18th century a type of hotplate was introduced. It consisted of a flat cast-iron plate set into a brick base. Round holes for cooking vessels were set into the hotplate. Underneath the hotplate was a fire box or fire boxes, depending on the model, with flues running under the hotplate to remove the fumes.

On February 27, 1802, George Bodley introduced the father of all kitchen ranges. The front of the fire was open and the heat was drawn through flues all round and over the top of the oven, where it heated the hotplate.

YORKSHIRE RANGE

The next development came at the beginning of the 19th century with the Yorkshire range. This was designed with a deep firebox enclosed in front with iron firebars. Upper bars could swing down to make a trivet for slow cooking and simmering. A set of hinged bars could be lowered over the fire itself to support pots and pans. The oven was on one side, and had a flue running underneath it, up the far side and over the top, so that the oven was heated on all sides. The space opposite the oven could house a small water tank for hot water, which was filled by hand, or it could be used as a low heat hob. There were, of course, a number of variations on this theme. The main weakness of the Yorkshire range was that the open grate used up fuel at a great rate and the heat was difficult to regulate.

*Kitchen scene, 1832. By permission of
the Radio Times Hulton Picture
Library.*

*Alexis Soyer's stove, 19th century. By
permission of the Radio Times Hulton
Picture Library.*

THE CLOSED 'KITCHENER' RANGE

The closed Kitchener range appeared about 1830. This was more of a cooking stove than a fire, as the fire box could be shut in front and the chimney opening sealed.

The Kitchener was popular in the Midlands and the South, while the Yorkshire range found favour in the North.

The principle of the Kitchener was that when it was required for cooking only, the fire box could be closed down so there was no direct or radiant heat, making it more efficient and certainly cooler for the cook. The design was in general similar to the Yorkshire range, except that the top of the fire was covered with a hotplate with removable boiling rings. The

SOYER'S MODERN HOUSEWIFE'S KITCHEN APPARATUS.

Containing an Open Roasting Fire, a Hot Water Boiler, a Baking Oven, a Broiling Stove, a Hot Plate, &c., all heated by one Fire.
Height 2ft. 4in., Width 2ft., Length 3ft.

hotplate slid back to open the fire for stoking. The front of the fire box normally had a door which was closed during cooking. There were two ovens, one on either side of the fire box and below the hotplate. If preferred an oven could be replaced by a water tank. Dampers helped control the rate of burning.

Even in the 19th century there was concern for smoke abatement, and a closed Kitchener made by Brown and Green of Luton was awarded the Gold Medal in the 1882 Smoke Abatement Exhibition.

PORTABLE STOVES

The Yorkshire and Kitchener ranges were the main types of appliances supplying both a cooking area and space-heating. There was however a range of freestanding portable stoves designed principally for cooking. This style of stove was popular in working-class houses as it was small, easy to run and cheap. The idea was introduced to this country in 1854 and was based on American portable stoves used by settlers.

One model was sold complete with two iron pots, a tea kettle, a potato strainer, a large ham boiler, two frying pans, a grid iron and eight iron baking tins, for an inclusive price of 78 shillings (£3.90). It sounds quite a bargain, but could easily have represented a month's wages for many workers at that time.

The advent of gas and then electricity in the latter part of the 19th century with independent appliances for cooking, space-heating and water-heating represented a novelty for the well-to-do, and didn't seriously interfere with the production of solid fuel equipment. Solid fuel ranges were already installed in most working-class homes and served the double rôle of supplying cosy heat and space for cooking, which was important as most houses were small and the family tended to live in the homely kitchen.

HEAT-STORAGE COOKERS

A considerable change in design came in the early 1930s with the introduction of the heat-storage cooker, such as the Aga and Esse.

The hotplates and ovens of these cookers were kept at a correct working temperature by heavy and efficient insulation with slag-wool. The hotplate heat was preserved by insulated, hinged covers which were only lifted when the hotplate was required for cooking.

In today's models the fire burns smokeless fuel and is thermostatically controlled, so the cooker is always ready for cooking. The oven has a thermometer. The lines have become more modern and the cooker is available in a choice of colours.

Heat-storage cookers can be fired by gas or oil, as well as solid fuel. There is an upper roasting oven at a higher temperature than the lower simmering oven. They also supply hot water.

GAS COOKERS

William Murdock, a Scot, was the first man to experiment with coal gas for domestic use. In 1779 he lit his home in Cornwall with gas which was stored in bladders.

The British were slow to accept gas as a cooking fuel. It was expensive when compared with coal; also it was difficult to measure consumption as there were no gas meters. Slot meters were not introduced until 1890.

The first gas cooker appeared around 1812. It was a basic piece of equipment looking rather like a coal range, and consisting of a number of cast-iron pieces making up an oven and two burner hotplates. There is no record that this cooker ever became a commercial proposition.

In 1824 a gas appliance made from a gun-barrel which was twisted into the shape of a grid-iron with a number of small holes pierced in it was made at the Aetna Iron Works near Liverpool. It was, in fact, the forerunner of the griller on our modern gas cookers.

To fry or boil, the gridiron was kept level and the pan placed on top; to roast, the gridiron was set vertical and the meat was hung in front of it. To speed up the roasting a 'hastener' was placed behind the meat (see page 21).

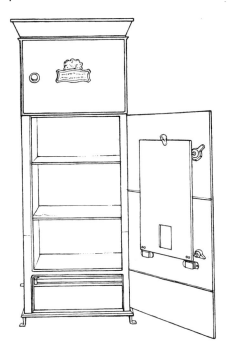

'Southampton' gas cooker, probably 1839–1840. By permission of Radiation Ltd.

The conversion to gas cooking took a step forward when Alexis Soyer, the famous French chef, introduced gas cooking appliances into the kitchens of the Reform Club, London, in 1841. Soyer claimed that gas stoves were more economical than coal as they were not lit until needed and could be turned off immediately the cooking was completed.

The mid-19th century saw the development of the gas cooker as we would recognise it today—a black cast-iron box-shaped contraption on four legs consisting of a hotplate with burners, a grill underneath the hotplate and an oven. These early cookers stood on stone slabs as a precaution against overheating the wooden kitchen floors.

The oven flue came out of the back of the oven and deposited the products of combustion, grease and grime, directly on to the wall behind the cooker.

'Camden' gas cooker, produced approximately 1890. By permission of Radiation Ltd.

The cook had to gauge the oven temperature by guesswork, but a browning sheet (a flat metal plate) was placed on the runners over the dish being cooked, and helped to concentrate the heat into a space suitable for the dish being cooked and also provided extra top browning. It in fact reduced the size of the oven. These early ovens were insulated with straw!

By 1896 gas as a fuel for domestic use was fully launched, and at least 70,000 gas appliances were in use in the London area alone.

20TH CENTURY

By the First World War, gas cookers were commonplace, and there were models to suit all pockets. Burners were more efficient, plate racks and small splashplates were general.

Gas cooker manufacturers began to realise that the housewife found the heavy black cast-iron appliance rather unattractive and difficult to clean. Unfortunately the 1914–18 war prevented any advance in the design of domestic equipment, and it wasn't until 1927 that a cream-enamel finished gas cooker was introduced, although as early as 1884 John Wright & Co. had purchased the patent rights of grey mottle stove enamel. However, some gas cookers had enamel spillage trays and side panels in the early 1920s. The first all-enamel cooker appeared in 1930.

OVEN THERMOSTATS

Work on temperature control began in 1919, and the first thermostatic oven control was introduced in 1923. By the 1930s this device was in common use and represented a substantial advance in oven design.

The basic principle is that a heat-sensitive element controls the rate of gas flow. Depending on the setting of the control knob, so the oven temperature is regulated, and as the limiting temperature set by the control knob is approached the gas valve closes. The valve must not close completely, otherwise the flame will go out.

The first heat-sensitive element used was a rod of a metal that does not expand on heating inside a tube made of a different metal which expands

'New World' gas cooker 1923. This model was the first ever Regulo cooker and an example is in the Science Museum, London. By permission of Radiation Ltd.

when hot. The rods are joined together at one end, and the inner rod attached to a valve in the thermostat head. The difference in the rate of thermal expansion causes the outer rod to pull down the inner rod, so closing the valve, as the oven reaches the required temperature. The movement of the valve adjusts the flow of gas to the burner.

The more recent type of thermostat depends on the expansion of a liquid in a phial at the end of a fine metal tube which is connected with the control valve in the same way as the inner part of the rod thermostat. In both instances the thermostat control knob is calibrated by numbers which relate to specific foods; the temperatures at which these foods cook best may vary according to the design of the oven, but this is only a matter of concern for the manufacturer. Whatever the design of the oven, the thermostat settings are the same, which simplifies recipe writing.

DISC BAR HOTPLATE

A further development in design was the introduction in 1930 of a disc bar hotplate which provided a stable surface for pans of all sizes. Immediately over the head of each burner was a metal disc which was integral with the main bars. This disc provided a firm base for small pans while the bars allowed large, heavy pans to be moved easily over the hotplate. The price of a Eureka New World in 1930 with a disc bar hotplate, oven Regulo and mottled enamel finish ranged from £7.30 to £23. The oven Regulo was extra on the model priced £7.30.

In 1933 glass oven doors appeared for the first time. The next trend was the cabinet-look. These were cookers with a hinged lid which covered the hotplate when not in use. One model not only had a shut-down lid but doors that enclosed the whole front of the cooker when not in use.

Cold catalytic hotplate ignition was introduced in 1937. However, it wasn't very reliable and was exchanged for the flash tube ignition from a central pilot light. In the same year heat-resisting grill frets were introduced, which allowed a more even spread of heat and greater speed in heating up for grilling.

The 1939–45 war prevented any further development of gas cooking equipment for the first year or so, but towards the end of the war, quite a lot of work went on to produce designs suitable for people being re-housed, and for the future.

THE POST-WAR SCENE

All cookers manufactured after the war had to comply with the recently published British Standard requirements.

The end of 1947 saw the introduction of a series to be built on a chassis like a car rather than of separate parts bolted together.

An important advance for the housewife came in 1950 when cooker manufacturers agreed to standardise their thermostat settings so that the same foods were cooked at the same mark whatever the make or model of cooker. Before this each manufacturer devised his own set of marks, and some even used letters.

One of the main design differences between the pre-war and the modern gas cooker is the position of the grill. Instead of being under the hotplate the grill now tends to be at high level. This was introduced in 1953, and during this year came a model with a high-level grill with automatic ignition of the grill and oven as well as to the hotplate.

From 1959 all gas cookers were made with automatic ignition on the hotplate, and many models at this date had press-button ignition on both oven and grill.

Another design feature was that gas cookers lost their legs and the space was utilised for a storage drawer or warming cupboard.

Oven door handles were streamlined and no longer prominent features.

Thermostatically controlled hotplates were introduced in 1959; these could be set to keep the food in a pan at any desired temperature indefinitely.

Rotisseries and spits were available on gas cookers from 1960. They are found today in the oven or as a grill attachment. The design of the spit is very similar to the pronged spit used by cooks in the Middle Ages (see pp. 18–23).

The early 1960s saw the co-operation between some cooker and some kitchen fitment manufacturers to produce a cooker which fitted in with the standard kitchen units. At this time there emerged a split-level cooker which had time control; and a two-section grill, which could be used either full on or heated only over half its area. Unfortunately this cooker was ahead of its time and had only limited appeal.

In 1960, a manufacturer, in collaboration with Watson House, the Gas Council's Research Station for research, development and approval of gas appliances, brought out the Gazoset clockwork time control device which gave gas cooker manufacturers the option of not including electrical time control devices on their cookers.

In 1971 spark ignition was introduced on cookers. It is powered by mains or battery electricity.

During the same year some cookers incorporated the 'Simmerset' tap, which provides a stable flame at a much lower gas rate than previously possible.

By the end of 1971 all new cookers were required to have flame failure devices on the oven burner. These cut off the supply of gas if there is no flame present to light it, and are used on many other gas appliances as well.

Oven cleaning is a major advance in labour-saving devices, and 1970 saw the introduction of a self-cleaning oven lining. The oven sides, back and top are coated with a 'continuous-clean' enamel which digests grease splashes all the time the oven is hot. Any excessive splashing can be removed by wiping the surface with a damp cloth and a liquid detergent.

NATURAL GAS

1966 saw the introduction of natural gas from the Sahara with the experiment at Canvey Island where all gas appliances were converted to burn Sahara gas. However, by the October of that year the first successful strike was made in the North Sea, and Great Britain was independent of the Sahara. The decision to alter the appliances to suit the natural gas meant that hundreds of different conversion sets needed to be designed and approved by the Gas Council. By the end of 1969 all appliances on the current Gas Council list had to be approved for both gases with the minimum of adjustment on conversion. As the conversion process goes on, 'natural gas only' appliances are now being approved.

ELECTRIC COOKERS

It was not until the 1880s that the first electric power station, The Holborn Viaduct Station, was opened to supply private consumers, although Sir Humphry Davy had demonstrated electric light at the Royal Institution in 1810.

The electric cooker didn't appear on the domestic scene until the late 1880s, and the first practical electric cookers were shown at the Electrical

Fair at the Crystal Palace in 1891. At the Chicago World's Fair in 1893 a model electric kitchen featured an electric range, electric broilers and kettles.

Colonel Crompton, the famous engineer, made electric cookers, and his company, Crompton & Co. of London, introduced his first electric cooker in 1895. Some of Crompton's appliances can be seen at the Science Museum, South Kensington, London.

EARLY APPLIANCES

Early electric appliances were plugged into an independent fascia over the oven with a battery of plugs and switches. The separate appliances stood on top of the oven or beside it on a table, or on the floor.

The following extract from an article published in January 1895 in an illustrated London journal gives a vivid description of a cookery demonstration using 'trained lightning' at the Gloucester Road School of Cookery. The writer reported that 'Miss Fairclough (the demonstrator) stood before it (the table) rolling pastry, while in front in a neat little row were six cooking utensils. All were bright shining copper and steel, from the kettle to the fluted griller, and they simply stood on the table without any fire or apparent sign of heat. Yet there on the griller was a chop cooking gaily away with an independent air; in the kettle water was boiling; on the hotplate scones were toasting; in a frying pan potatoes were frying; while two little pots were occupied stewing bird and simmering jam.'

By 1905 several types of electric cookers were available. A large number of these early cookers were in fact based on gas cooker carcasses, but with boiling plates and oven elements taking the place of gas burners.

Around 1910 A. E. Berry of the British Transformer Co. (to become the Tricity Co.) had so publicised electric cooking that some 10,000 electric ovens were in use. About this time a cooker with a glass oven door was introduced. In the Science Museum you can see a model of a 1913 Jackson cooker with a glass oven door.

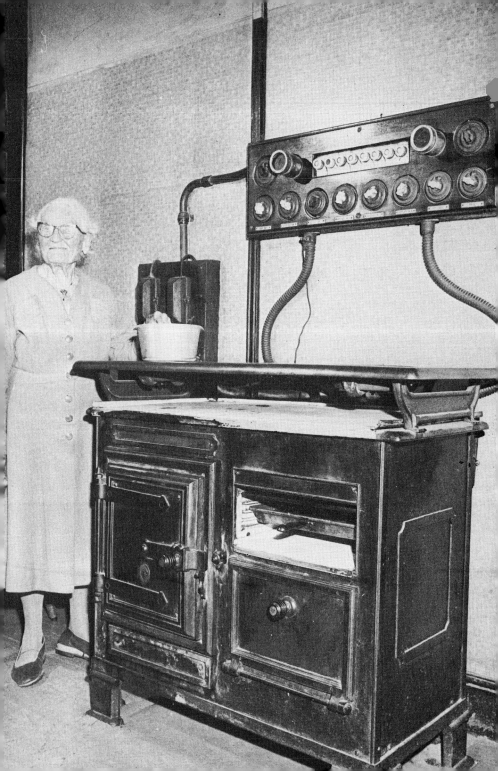

Miss Alice Rogers of Croydon, pictured with the Cannon electric cooker which was installed in her family home in 1900. Over seventy years later it is still in perfect working order, and though, as Miss Rogers now lives alone, a smaller cooker is better suited to her needs, she still uses the big one occasionally for special batches of baking. By permission of the Electricity Council.

An all electric kitchen, 1908. By permission of the Radio Times Hulton Picture Library.

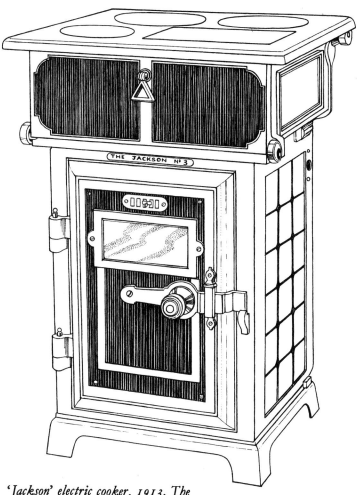

THE JACKSON Nº 3

'*Jackson' electric cooker, 1913. The*
oven door has a glass viewing panel.
By permission of Radiation Ltd.

CONSERVATIVE PUBLIC

The British public were conservative in their approach to this new element and its advantages. The electric cooker didn't become really popular until the 1930s, by which time power had been installed in country areas as well as in the towns. Mr. C. R. Belling did a lot to advance the popularity of electricity as a cooking medium when he introduced, in the mid-1920s, a new, smaller type of electric cooker. These were small table models, usually with a small oven and single boiling plate, which doubled as a grill and top oven element.

FINISHES AND STYLING

The first cookers were built in black cast iron. Running almost parallel with gas cooker development, the first vitreous enamelled electric cooker appeared in 1931, although enamelled panels and splash trays under the hotplate had been available since the 1920s.

In 1938 the first cabinet style electric cookers were produced. On these cookers the body came right down to the floor, rather than being a box-like structure mounted on legs. This was considered a major design advance. Coloured enamel finishes, usually green and cream, began to appear.

HOTPLATES

The main disadvantage of the electric cooker in the early days was that the hotplates took a long time to heat up and once heated up to cool down again; while gas, as M. Soyer aptly remarked, could be instantly turned on and off.

The elements which heated the early hotplates were coils of wire attached to fireclay moulds. These elements were covered with a piece of heavy cast iron. The heat generated by the coils had to pass through the solid metal before it reached the pan. As the hotplates tended to take a long time to cool down after use, the housewife thought she was wasting valuable heat—which she was!

Consequently the early days of promoting electric cookers were concerned with advising the housewife on how she could use this residual heat to her advantage. This was obviated in 1935 with the introduction of quick heating, tubular boiling rings as an alternative to the heavy cast-iron hotplates. This was a considerable improvement.

CONTROLS

Initially the control of heat was limited to a choice of three heat settings— high, medium and low. Present-day cookers are fitted with much more variable controls.

OVENS

The ovens of electric cookers always had a thermometer on the outside of the door. But as the control knob only registered 'high', 'medium' and 'low' settings, the housewife had the inconvenience of switching the oven up or down as the cooking temperature fell or rose. For the busy house-wife the launching of a thermostatically controlled oven in 1937 must have been a boon. This was based on the same principle as the thermostat available on the gas oven (see page 48).

Glass oven doors also became a common feature at this time.

The outbreak of the Second World War in 1939 brought all development to a standstill until the early 1950s, when domestic equipment evolved rapidly.

POST-WAR DEVELOPMENTS

THE HOB

The main developments to date on the hob are: *Radiant rings* with a coil that glows red. These are almost universal today. In *disc rings* the coil element is enclosed in a case of lightweight metal. Disc rings are now mainly used for split level worktops.

The dual ring or two-in-one ring is divided into two coils which are separately switched. This was first seen in 1969. It can be used as a normal boiling ring, or just the smaller central coil can be heated up separately, thus saving electricity when using a small based pan.

The pan-sensing thermostat which keeps the temperature of the contents of a pan constant at any chosen setting was introduced in 1960.

The device is a spring-loaded disc set in the middle of the boiling ring. The disc makes contact with the base of the pan and automatically takes its temperature throughout the cooking period, so that once the control knob has been turned to the appropriate setting the sensing disc will keep the temperature of the pan's contents constant.

The ceramic hob is a major development which was first seen in prototype in 1971. It is made of very tough, heat-resistant opaque glass. The completely flat, smooth surface has the heating elements set underneath. The heated areas on the hob are patterned for identification. These areas can become very hot but the surrounding area remains cool. The advantages are a large pan area and ease of cleaning, also the ceramic hob is visually extremely attractive.

The Cool-Top hob is a method of heating food on a cool surface. It was demonstrated for the first time in early 1972. It consists of a flat ceramic hob with cooking points marked out as rings. It works by induction heating; a wire coil beneath the cooker top produces an oscillating magnetic field which induces an eddy current in a metal cooking vessel placed on the cooker. For example a pan of water can be brought to the boil with a piece of paper between it and the Cool-Top hob. When the paper is removed it is cool and there is no sign of scorching. It is reckoned that this cooker will cost in the region of £800.

THE GRILL

Because of the greater use of the grill in modern cooking, there has been a tendency to increase the grilling area considerably, until now when many grills have twice the cooking area of those available a few years ago.

Some of these larger grills have split level elements, so that one half can be switched off when cooking smaller meals.

Generally electric cookers have waist-level grills situated under the hob, although some models have high-level grills placed at the top of the backplate.

On some high-level models there is an enclosed griller compartment which also contains a rotating, motor-driven spit. In some instances a second, separately controlled element is fitted in the compartment so that it can be used as a small cool oven for the slow cooking of such dishes as casseroles or milk puddings.

The grilling compartment on some waist-level models is fitted with an element at the bottom which converts the compartment into a small, second oven. The more modern types are thermostatically controlled and linked to the autotimer.

CLEAN OVENS

The greatest post-war development in electric oven design and convenience for the housewife has been in the cleaning field.

For many years the interior finish was vitreous enamel which could withstand attack from acids and alkalis found in food spillage and in domestic oven cleaning materials.

The next step was the removable oven lining which made cleaning easier in that the liner could be taken to the kitchen sink for washing. This surface however required fairly rigorous cleaning, usually aided by caustic oven-cleaning materials, unless wiped over after every use.

NON-STICK LININGS

The introduction of non-stick removable linings of coated polytetra-fluorethylene (PTFE) was a considerable advance in easy clean surfaces (see manufacturing process page 30). These linings were available on a British cooker in 1968 as an optional extra at the time of purchase. The price of a set of linings was around £7 which brought ease of cleaning within the range of everyone.

PTFE is both moisture and dirt repellent. Splashes of fat from roasting food stick to the linings in small globules rather than spreading out as happens with vitreous enamel. In consequence only a small area is soiled. PTFE coated linings require no more than a quick sponging with warm water and a mild detergent to clean. Any persistent stains may require soaking for a short time.

The non-stick lining allows the housewife an easily cleaned surface at a reasonable cost, bridging the economic gap between the traditional vitreous enamelled oven finish and the sophisticated auto-clean oven.

SELF-CLEANING OVENS

A British made autoclean oven was launched in 1968. This oven is cleaned by the 'pyrolitic' method developed in America. It works by carbonising or burning all the splashes and spills to a fine grey ash by the raising of the interior oven temperature to a very high temperature of 900° F (482° C). The ash can be wiped or swept out at the end of the operation.

The door of the autoclean oven is safety locked once the oven has risen above normal bake temperature, and can't be opened until the operation is completed, which includes time for cooling down to about 500° F (240° C). The cleaning process lasts between two and three hours and at the time of writing costs about 2½p a time.

The meat pan, side runners, deflector plate, grill pan and the removable spillage bowls from under the hob in some models can be cleaned by leaving them in the oven during the self-cleaning process.

The autocleaning cooker is expensive, costing in the region of £110 to £129.

CATALYTIC ENAMELS

In 1970, oven parts coated with catalytic enamel were introduced. This enamel is virtually self-cleaning in that most of the fat splashes are burnt off as they occur.

The great advantage of this system, known as Cook Clean or Stay Clean, is that the oven is always available for cooking as cleaning is a continuous cycle, not a special operation, and that it is comparatively cheap. Some major electric cooker manufacturers include Cook Clean parts at no extra cost. One model has the grill compartment treated with this finish.

AUTOTIMER

The automatic oven control or autotimer allows the housewife more independence. With this device, which works in conjunction with the electric clock built into the control panel, the housewife can set the oven to turn itself on and off automatically at selected times. This means that the housewife can prepare a meal, say supper, put it in the oven, set the timing device and go out for the day knowing that the meal will be cooked or cooking by the time she returns. The first autotimer controlled electric cooker was launched in 1954.

FAN-ASSISTED OVENS

1971 saw the fan-assisted or forced-air circulation oven incorporated into a domestic cooker for the first time. The type of oven is already in use in the catering trade.

A fan drives heated air round the oven, so that every section of the oven is heated to the same even temperature. This allows batches of cakes or bread or pastries to be cooked to the same even consistency and colour on any shelf in the oven. Not only does this give greater cooking space for the experienced cook, but it removes the problem of which shelf to cook on for the inexperienced housewife.

There is less shrinkage of meat, and cooking times are slightly reduced. As the oven is also less heavily loaded than that of a conventional cooker, there is an overall economy in use.

MICROWAVE OVENS

Microwave cooking is a new method of cooking in that it does not use fire in any way to cook the food. Conventional cooking by solid fuel, gas or electricity makes use of heat transference, whereas microwave cooking makes use of electronic energy.

Development on an electronic tube to produce microwave energy began in 1941 in Birmingham. Its use was for defence purposes in the Second World War.

Although the first microwave cooker was produced in America in the late 1940s, it didn't appear in this country until 1959; and was for commercial use in hotels, hospitals, restaurants and snack bars.

Food cooked by microwave is bombarded by electro-magnetic waves (very high frequency radio waves). These create energy within the food which generates heat and causes the food to become heated through in a very short time. The heat is produced within the food itself and not conducted from an outside source.

The microwaves don't brown food, so it is not a good method of cooking foods which by tradition need a crisp brown surface for eye appeal. For instance, a steak so cooked would still have to be put under a conventional grill to make it acceptable.

Its greatest advantage today is for reheating precooked food in the catering trade. The food is cooked, plated up and refrigerated by the chef. It can be reheated, at a later stage, in the microwave oven direct from the refrigerator by unskilled staff or the customer in a matter of minutes.

OVEN THERMOSTAT MARKINGS GO METRIC

A change which will affect everybody is metrication. It is expected that Britain will be using metric measurements in the home by 1975. It is proposed that thermostats on electric ovens, at present calibrated in 25° F divisions, will be calibrated in 10° C.

When the change occurs conversion charts will be readily available.

Overleaf are figures published by the Association of Manufacturers of Domestic Electrical Appliances which give temperature equivalents for oven thermostat markings:

PROPOSED TABLE OF TEMPERATURE EQUIVALENTS FOR OVEN THERMOSTAT MARKINGS

°F	°C	°F	°C
150	70	350	180
175	80	375	190
200	100	400	200
225	110	425	220
250	130	450	230
275	140	475	240
300	150	500	250
325	170		

Examples: Two commonly used settings are 350° F and 425° F. In metric terms these become 180° C (i.e. 356° F) and 220° C (i.e. 428° F).

OIL

Brief mention must be made of oil cookers, but they have never secured more than a slender foothold in the British home.

Oil cookers were introduced in America in about 1880, due to the prolific oil wells of Pennsylvania. Oil was and still is, no doubt, used in the outlying country districts of America, Canada, and in parts of Britain.

FURTHER READING

Home Fires Burning. Lawrence Wright. Routledge & Kegan Paul Ltd, 1964.

Kitchen and Table. Colin Clair. Abelard Schuman, 1964.

The Story of the Kitchen. S. E. Ellacott. Methuen, 1953.

Food in England. Dorothy Hartley. Macdonald, 1954.

Solid Fuel and Combustion Appliance Review. Supplement to the *Coal Merchant and Shipper.* November 6, 1954; May 1, 1954.

Electric Cookers. Gwen Conacher. Forbes Publications Ltd, 1971.

Easy Clean Ovens. Barbara Hanforth. *Home Economics,* May 1969.

Why Microwave? Stephanie Blasberg. *Home Economics,* November 1969.

Programmed Cooking. Jean Whitgift. *Home Economics,* March and April 1966.

The Mystery of Mircrowave. Stephanie Blasberg. *Home Economics,* February and April 1972.

3 The Table

TABLE TRADITIONS

The story of tableware mirrors the changing social scene. Tastes and customs in food, drink and the service of meals have had a tremendous influence on the variety of 'pieces' in use on the table at different periods of our history.

As life became more secure and leisurely, so manners and table customs changed and improved. This brought about a slow and gradual progress in the design and the function of tableware, which developed with the tastes and needs of the time.

The shapes have remained basically the same, although materials used for tableware have changed and customs altered. This is because the materials used are malleable, such as clay, glass and metals, which naturally adopt a curved or rounded shape when worked, or which can be easily moulded.

MEDIEVAL POMP

The preparation of the table, though simple, and the service of the meal, was bound by rigorous ceremony in the great houses.

Dinner, the principal meal of the day, was usually taken between 11 and 12 o'clock. Supper, a light repast, was eaten around 6 p.m.

Dinner was an important event in that the whole household, including servants and retainers, was gathered together, and it was the one time in the day when any news or information could be exchanged. It was also a time for relaxation, enjoyment and pleasure in a dangerous age. Food was the staff of life; it was a precious and hard-worked-for commodity and, therefore, warranted certain ceremony.

Meals were served in the great hall which was modestly furnished with a dresser or 'cup board', tables and benches. The dining table consisted of two or three long boards laid on trestles. The permanent table, as we understand it today, came into fashion during the end of the 15th century.

The master of the house, his family and guests sat at the top or high table which was raised on a dais at the end of the hall, while ordinary folk, servants and retainers sat at long tables placed below the top table.

Backless benches or stools were the rule for all but royalty, high dignitaries, and the master of the house, who would have used a primitive high-backed chair.

Although the laying of the table and the service of food was accompanied by ceremony, with young men or boys of the household having a specific job to do in the ritual, the medieval table was totally practical, carrying only what was essential to the meal. (The giving of household duties to boys of notable families was a way of teaching the practical niceties of life.) The Great Salt Cellar supplied any decoration necessary, and was the most important article on the table.

The Salt set the social order of the day. The master of the household sat in the middle of the top table and the Salt was set before him. When guests were present the Salt was moved down the table so that the host and honoured guests sat above the Salt and ordinary folk sat below. In medieval books of courtesy or etiquette there are special references to salt and table manners.

TUDOR FASHIONS

Life at table during the Tudor and Stuart times became more comfortable. The benches were replaced by padded and cushioned stools. Glass was replacing wooden, pewter and leather drinking vessels. The great hall was declining, while the family, unless entertaining lavishly, inclined more and more to take their meals in privacy. The protocol, however, was just as rigorous.

THE PLACE-SETTING

Until the mid-1600s the place-setting didn't change very much. Each diner was served with a trencher (see page 73) and supplied his own spoon and knife. There were no table forks.

Food was placed on the table in large dishes and everyone served himself, putting the food onto his trencher. The fingers were used for serving and eating the food. The knife was used for taking a cut from the roast, and the spoon for soup and dessert.

A TIME FOR CHANGE

The major change in eating habits came gradually during the 17th century with the evolution of a new moneyed class, and growing political stability which helped to increase economic prosperity, all of which contributed to the upsurge in lavish entertainment. It was the age of the bourgeois who needed to display his material success.

A vivid picture of life during this period can be gleaned from Pepys' diaries. He was an observer of the minutiae of domestic life.

MEAL TIMES

Breakfast was now served between 9.30 and 10 a.m. It was a more substantial meal and it became fashionable to hold breakfast parties. Dinner began to move forwards from noon to between 3 and 5 o'clock, though some households dined even later. Tea tended to be served after dinner, rather as we now serve coffee.

A light, informal supper might be provided before people went to bed. Or, if there had been an early dinner, say, at 2 o'clock, tea might be served 3 or 4 hours later, in which case supper might be dispensed with. Meal times were much more flexible and arranged to suit individual families or circumstances.

SERVICE OF MEALS

The service of meals became more sophisticated. Instead of several meats or a whole course being served together on a single, large platter, each dish was served separately on its own covered container by a servant to each diner, or placed on the table, so that the table was covered with a number of dishes, looking rather like the buffet service of today.

During the late 18th century this fashion changed and there developed a set pattern for the placing of dishes.

In my 1786 edition of *The Experienced English Housekeeper*, by Mrs. Elizabeth Raffald, there are directions and two layouts for a Grand Table.

You will see in the illustration an 18th century dinner of two courses. The first course was laid on the table with two 'removes' (in this case a fish remove and a haunch of venison). All the other dishes were known as 'dormants'. The removes were taken away after a specific time and replaced by two new dishes. The dormants remained on the table.

Then the whole table was cleared and the second course appeared, to be followed by dessert. This fashion was known as 'à la Française'.

At a very elaborate dinner party as many as four or five separate courses might be served. The diners helped themselves, the men carving for the women. The same plate was used for all the dishes.

(*Overleaf*)
'Layout' of first and second courses of an 18th-century dinner. From The Experienced English Housekeeper *by Elizabeth Raffald, published 1736. Elizabeth Raffald had been housekeeper to Lady Elizabeth Warburton— evidently a position of some importance, and her frontispiece portrait shows her as a dignified lady in a silk gown and lace-trimmed cap.*

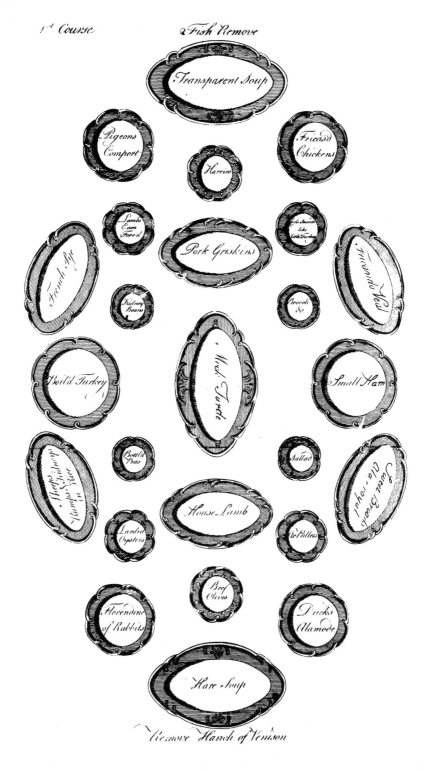

1st Course.   Fish Remove

Transparent Soup

Pigeons Comport

Fricas'd Chickens

Harrico

Lambs Ears Forc'd

Sweet Breads like Little Turkey

Pork Griskins

French Pye

Fricando Veal

Kidney Beans

Brocoli &c

Boil'd Turkey

Mock Turtle

Small Ham

Sheeps Kidneys & Rumps &c in Slices

Bottld Peas

Sallad

Sweet Breads Old = rowel

House Lamb

Larded Oysters

Ye Pallets

Beef Olives

Florendine of Rabbits

Ducks Alamode

Hare Soup

Remove Haunch of Venison

Pheasant

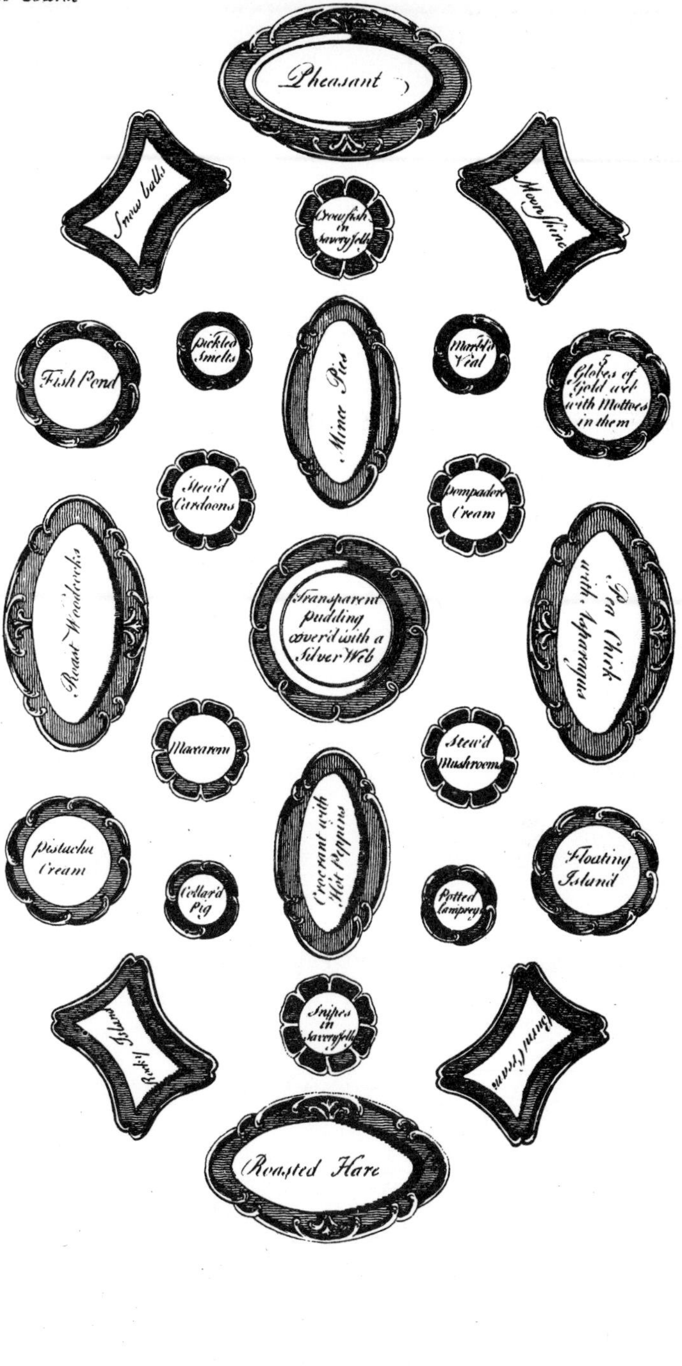

Snow balls

Moon Shine

Crawfish in savery Jelly

Fish Pond

Pickled Smelts

Minc'd Pies

Marbled Veal

Globes of Gold web with Mottoes in them

Stew'd Cardoons

Pompadore Cream

Roast Woodcocks

Transparent pudding cover'd with a Silver Web

Pea Chick with Asparagus

Macaroni

Stew'd Mushrooms

Pistachia Cream

Crocant with Hot Poppins

Floating Island

Collar'd Pig

Potted lampreys

Rocky Island

Snipes in savery Jelly

Burnt Cream

Roasted Hare

In the mid-19th century the uncluttered table as we know it today made its debut. It was known as 'à la Russe'. Every single dish of each course was removed from the table, except for the place-settings of china, silver and glass, candlesticks and flowers.

These changes and developments didn't happen overnight. As the country's economic prosperity developed and leisure increased, so this new attitude to the art of the kitchen and pleasure of the table grew, until it culminated in the extravaganza of Victorian and Edwardian England, declining again to our own rather practical attitude towards food and its presentation.

'A state party', 1861 by Richard Doyle. By permission of the Radio Times Hulton Picture Library.

BIRD'S-EYE VIEWS OF SOCIETY.   No. IV.

"A State Party."

But a point always to remember is that these changes applied to the prosperous classes. The poor continued to live much as they had always done from hand to mouth, with no time, money or energy for gracious living.

DISHES FOR THE TABLE

A medieval table-setting would look very meagre to our eyes (see page 67). Each diner was served with a hunk of bread, known as a trencher which acted as a plate. He might hollow out the centre of the bread to hold more meat and collect any gravy.

'The Dinner Party' from My First Season—The Graphic, *24 April 1890. By permission of the Radio Times Hulton Picture Library.*

*Banquet in the 11th century. By
permission of the Radio Times Hulton
Picture Library.*

Bread used for trenchers had to be four days old and it was cut to a
particular size and thickness.

WOOD

Wooden platters and bowls of various shapes and sizes were used for the
service of food both in ordinary and in wealthy households. It was a
handy, cheap, easy-to-work and durable commodity.

Wooden trenchers began to appear in the early 1500s. They were usually
square in shape and some had a small hollow at one side to hold salt.

In the 16th and 17th centuries small bread and fruit trenchers, known as 'roundels', were made of beech or sycamore. On the underside of these trenchers was painted a short verse which was sung or read out at the end of the meal. From this custom, it is said, comes the word 'roundelay', meaning a song in which the refrain is repeated.

Wooden trenchers or 'plate trenchers', as they became known, were still in use in the middle of the 17th century. The change from trencher to platter occurred about this time when the square corners of the trencher were cut away, leaving a circular platter. In wealthy households the wooden platter was soon superseded by silver, pewter, and later by china and pottery.

POTTERY

Pottery didn't make a positive appearance at the dining table until the mid-18th century, although some was made during the Roman occupation and some during medieval times. A simple English slipware was made during the 17th century. It was a coarse earthenware with different coloured slips or bands of colour trailed over the dish or pot to produce a decoration. Most of this ware was used in the kitchen or dairy, though no doubt some found its way to the table.

There was a tremendous leap forward in 1736 when Josiah Wedgwood discovered a method of making earthenware with a cream body and a rich durable glaze which was cheap and easy to manufacture in bulk.

He described it as 'a species of earthenware for the table, quite new in appearance, covered with a rich and brilliant glaze, bearing sudden alterations of heat and cold, manufactured with ease and expedition, and consequently cheap'.

It was later to become known as Queen's Ware at the request of Queen Charlotte. It brought a tableware within the reach of all but the poor, and was a major development in the changing pattern of eating and service of food.

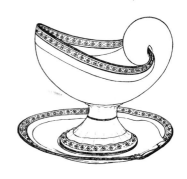

Silver cup, late 15th century, by permission of the Victoria and Albert Museum.

Sauce tureen and stand, Nautilus shape, Queen's Ware, late 18th century. By permission of The Wedgwood Group.

Tureen stand and cover in Queen's Ware, with hand-painted decoration in 'laurel' pattern from Josiah Wedgwood's first pattern book. By permission of The Wedgwood Group.

'Queen's Sprays' on Queen's Ware tea service. The design, still in use, was created by Josiah Wedgwood for Queen Charlotte in 1765. By permission of The Wedgwood Group.

Oak jug with iron staves, about 18th century. By permission of the University of Reading (Museum of English Rural Life).

THE SERVICE

The mid-18th century saw the rapid expansion of the pottery industry. An important result of this growth was the introduction of the *service*, which consisted of matching plates, cups and saucers for breakfast, dinner and tea.

By the 1800s the pottery industry in Britain was well on the way to industrialisation as we understand it today. The continuing development of the industry was due to the economic boom during the 19th century, the affluence of the middle classes and the scarcity of commercial amusements, which caused the well-to-do to pass their time in coffee-houses, clubs, gaming saloons and lavish entertainment at home. The pottery industry had a captive market for its wares, which was reflected in sumptuously loaded tables and in the decorations of many fancily shaped dishes used for entertainment. Families were large. Do you remember the many relatives of the Forsyte family in the *Forsyte Saga*? And so dinner services were in proportion. Many contained over 200 pieces.

PRESENT DAY

The trend today is the reduction of pieces in a range. This rationalisation of ranges has been introduced to make factory work more efficient and so cut the cost of the finished article to the consumer without loss of quality.

An example of this is the interchangeability of tableware. A designer when planning a new range thinks of the general purpose of the tableware throughout the day, instead of thinking in terms of a dinner service or a coffee set in isolation from each other. Teaplates can be used as soup-cup stands or as side plates at dinner; the sugar bowl is common to both tea and coffee ware; so are the saucers; the coffee cups are large and look as well on the all-purpose saucer as do the tea cups; a coffee jug doubles for a hot-water jug; so the 62 pieces in a tea-set, coffee-set and dinner service are reduced to some 39 pieces.

PORCELAIN AND CHINA

The Portuguese introduced porcelain in quantity to Europe from the East in the early 16th century, although a little Chinese porcelain had been brought to Europe by the Arabs as early as the 12th century. Because of its beauty and rarity, porcelain was treated as a treasure for display rather than use.

There were many years of experimentation before porcelain was first produced in Europe. The first factory was established at Meissen, Saxony, in 1710. However, it wasn't until the 1740s that porcelain was made in England. The earliest piece is claimed to be a Chelsea jug of 1745.

ENGLISH PORCELAIN

On the continent, porcelain factories were mainly owned by royalty, while in England they were developed privately. Early factories, such as Chelsea, Bow and Derby made tea and dinner services of exquisite beauty.

Early English porcelain tended to crack when boiling water was poured onto it, but in 1749 at a Bristol factory, later transferred to Worcester to become part of the Worcester Royal Porcelain Company, it was dis-covered that if soapstone was added to porcelain it made the fabric more resistant to sudden changes of temperature—it no longer cracked or crazed when hot liquids were used—so it became the ideal material for tea services.

BONE CHINA

In the early 19th century came the development of bone china with its pure white translucent body and brilliant glaze.

Bone china is so called because the 'ingredients' include calcinated animal bone (bone-ash) which causes complex chemical and physical changes during firing and results in the characteristic strength, translucency and whiteness. British china today is made to a standard mix of 50 per cent bone-ash.

Bone china was perfected by Josiah Spode, and this brought about a gradual decline in the porcelain industry except for expensive pieces of tableware.

RECENT DEVELOPMENTS

In 1932 the Worcester Royal Porcelain Company introduced porcelain oven-to-tableware, and in 1968 further developments resulted in the launching of true porcelain tableware which is light in weight, is resistant to heat and extremes of temperature, and is inexpensive. This tableware can be used both on top of the stove and in the oven. The manufacturer claims that dishes containing food can be taken straight from the home freezer and put immediately into a micro-wave oven (see page 62) without damage.

Royal Doulton first marketed English Translucent china in 1966. This is finer and stronger than earthenware, not as delicate as bone china, but cheaper.

POINTS TO NOTE

The main ceramic materials in use today are earthenware, stoneware, porcelain, bone china, and English Translucent china.

Earthenware is opaque and is porous under the glaze so that when it is chipped it will absorb moisture, and stain. This makes it unhygienic when cracked.

Stoneware is tougher and harder than earthenware and is generally used for oven-to-table ware. It is vitrified and does not absorb moisture when chipped.

Porcelain is a vitreous ceramic made translucent by its method of manufacture. It tends to be expensive.

Bone china—its main characteristics are strength and durability, coupled with whiteness and translucency. It is usually cheaper than porcelain.

English Translucent china—its method of manufacture provides a finer and stronger body than earthenware, but it is cheaper than bone china.

METALS

Copper, bronze and iron have been used in some form for centuries.

Pewter has been used in Britain since the Roman occupation. It was popular in the 14th century in wealthy homes, when it was mainly used in the kitchen, though some appeared at table in the form of serving dishes. The craft of making pewter domestic ware was at its height during the 17th and early 18th centuries.

Pewter was superseded by *Britannia metal* in the mid-18th century. Britannia metal, more malleable than pewter, was used for domestic holloware and cutlery and was much in demand at the end of the 18th century as a cheap substitute for silver.

Silver, a precious metal, was the prerogative of the rich, who kept it rather as an investment than for use at the table during the Middle Ages. By the 16th century, silver tableware was often gilded—known as silver gilt.

As the art of the table evolved and Britain prospered, much more silverware appeared on the table in the shape of cutlery, tea and coffee services, dishes in various shapes and sizes, cruets and elaborate centre-pieces for decoration of the table. Silver design was simple and elegant during the Georgian period, becoming more and more extravagant as the affluence of the Victorian era increased.

Coffee and breakfast set in stainless steel, 1968. By permission of the Stainless Steel Development Association.

Stainless steel goblet, 1971. By permission of the Stainless Steel Development Association.

The discovery of *Sheffield plate* in 1743 by Thomas Bolsover, a cutler's apprentice in Sheffield, brought 'silver' table appointments within the reach of the middle and working class families. Sheffield plating is a method of finely soldering silver onto base metal.

The development of *stainless steel* (also see kitchen ware page 28) in the 20th century brought about a further evolution in tableware. Here was a metal that didn't tarnish and kept its good looks without the effort of polishing. It was inexpensive, yet sophisticated enough in design to appeal to every type of household.

In the latter part of the 19th century dessert knives and forks and fish knives and forks were *electro-plated on nickel silver* (EPNS). It was considerably cheaper than silver and had many of the advantages. Today the quality of EPNS depends on the thickness of silver plating. A 1 is the best quality. Good quality EPNS can be a handsome, hardwearing and inexpensive substitute for silver.

PLASTICS

Plastics first appeared on the table in the 1930s. One type of thermoset plastic which is currently used for tableware is rigid, light in weight, resistant to all chemicals in domestic use today, and will withstand high temperatures. Another is claimed to be stain proof as well as being unbreakable, chip and crack-proof. Almost every month sees the production of new types with improved appearance; colours, in particular, are now far less crude than in the early examples.

GLASS

It is believed that the ancient Egyptians discovered the secrets of glass-making, but it was the Romans who brought it to this country. When the Romans left Britain the glass-making industry declined until its revival in the 13th century. By the 17th century it was again a flourishing industry, and fine decorative techniques had been evolved.

An important development during the latter part of the 17th century was the discovery by George Ravenscroft of a new type of glass which included oxide of lead instead of lime in its manufacture. This prevented the formation of internal cracks during manufacture and gave a particular brilliance to the glass. These two qualities plus the fact that the glass was softer, made it highly suitable for cutting and polishing.

The glass tax, levied in 1745 and assessed according to weight, was responsible for the development of decoration. Until this time the value of glass tended to be dictated by weight, now the beauty of design and cutting, engraving gilding and enamelling, dictated value.

From the 18th century the glass industry was mainly concerned with developing design and varieties of shapes to suit the new fashions in entertainment.

Domestic glass continued to be hand-blown until the 1930s, when the pressing of glass in moulds was introduced, first by hand and then automatically. This helped to bring table glass within the means of everybody.

Today, most glassware is made by automatic or semi-automatic mass production methods.

The main types of table glass made today are:

lead crystal which is most often used for tableware today;

soda-lime glass which is either made by machine or hand blown. It lacks the brilliance and weight of lead crystal. Soda-lime glass is all purpose—it can either be used for very cheap, mass production glass, or for making good quality table glassware.

FASHIONS IN DRINKING VESSELS

Drinking vessels of the Middle Ages include beakers, goblets, mazers, wassail bowls which were either enormous or goblet size, standing cups which were larger than goblets and mainly for ceremonial purposes, and tankards.

The materials commonly used were wood, pewter, leather, and horn which is not found as a drinking vessel after the 15th century. Imported glass was available but used for special occasions.

Earthenware jugs were used in the kitchen and buttery of large houses.

A mazer was a shallow, simply turned, thin wooden vessel, usually without a stem, made from mazer wood which is a generic term for close-grained woods, such as maple. In the 17th century the true English mazers died out and their place was taken by deeper bowls, with or without stems but still in wood.

Pewter tankards and beakers were popular in the 15th and 16th centuries.

Drinking vessels of the Middle Ages were under the care of the cup-bearer and were kept on the cup board. Anybody who wanted a drink had to ask the cup-bearer, who filled it with wine or mead and brought it to the table. When it was empty the cup was given back to the cup-bearer who washed it out and returned it to the cup board. This ritual would most likely have applied to the top table only. Servants and retainers would no doubt dip into a communal bowl or bucket of ale or beer.

GLASS VESSELS

By 1620 glass for the table was being mentioned in the inventories of large houses. The middle years of the 17th century saw the sacrifice of many silver and other precious vessels to the cause of the Civil War, and so, of necessity, English-made glassware began to take its place on the table.

The wine glass as we recognise it today with a bowl, stem and foot is believed to have been designed by a Venetian during the 16th century.

Records show us that during the latter part of the 17th century the well-to-do placed orders for beer, French wine and sack glasses in the same design. Was this the beginning of suites or sets of glasses as we know them today?

The increase in the production of wine glasses during the early part of the 18th century was due to the new process of including oxide of lead in glass manufacture and, in part, by the requirements of society which demanded regular supplies of glassware in keeping with the development of leisure and the consequent entertainment on a lavish scale. This necessitated sets of glasses of various sizes for ale, strong beer, different kinds of wines and potent waters.

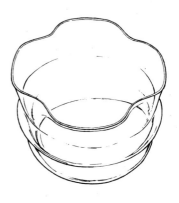

Group of glasses designed by Philip Webb in 1859.

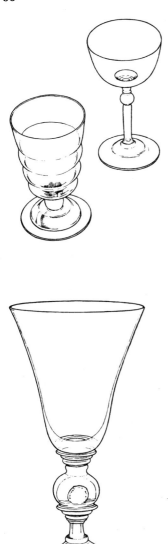

Goblet, clear glass with sixpence of William III embedded in stem. Late 17th century.

Goblet, clear glass with the seal of a raven's head, the emblem used by George Ravenscroft, 1676–1681.

By permission of the Victoria and Albert Museum.

Table glasses of the 18th century can be divided basically into three main sizes—the largest for beer and other long drinks, medium for wine and punch, and the smallest for cordial drinks.

The wine glass of the 18th century was smaller than earlier types due to wine being bottled and brought to table, rather than being drawn directly from the wood as in previous periods.

The champagne glass was introduced in about 1730.

By the 19th century the variety and design of table glass increased with the number and variety of wines drunk. Glass was now no longer a luxury but also a utility article which was cheap enough to be available to most middleclass households.

During the 18th to the mid-19th century there were some thirty-four different types of drinking glasses. Today a complete suite of glass would include glasses for champagne, brandy, gin and tonic, goblet, liqueur, port, red wine, white wine (long-stemmed), sherry, and tumblers for a long drink. This can be simplified to a four-glass set composed of a small glass for liqueurs, sherries, port, etc.; medium size for gin and tonic, champagne (the French serve champagne in tall glasses in preference to the open type) and wine; a large glass for long drinks, and a tumbler.

TOOLS FOR THE TABLE

The history of cutlery, or flatware as it is known in the trade, gives a vivid picture of man's social manners. The knife, fork and spoon evolved independently of each other, and the place-setting of knife, fork and spoon did not come together as an entity on the dining table until the late 17th century.

THE KNIFE

The knife is the oldest implement of the three, progressing from a blade of flint or obsidian to metal in the Bronze age. Flint blades were on the whole only practical for scraping and scratching. The bronze blade marked a considerable advance in man's domestic culture. He now had a tool with which he could cut his meat from the bone.and then carry it to his mouth

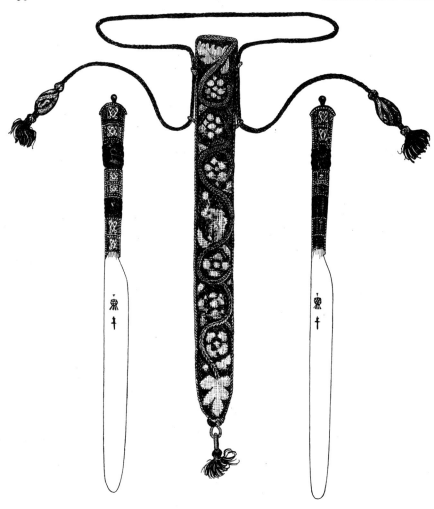

*Pair of knives with sheath, the
handles of iron damascened with gold
and encrusted with silver, and set with
panels of faceted amber. By permission
of the Victoria and Albert Museum.*

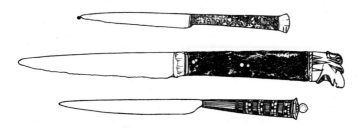

Knife, mid 16th century
Knife, early 16th century
Knife, late 16th century (*Italian*)

on the knife's point, rather than tearing at his food with his teeth and hands.

The knife, until the 14th century, was all-purpose, probably used for fighting and eating, carving and scraping. So, of necessity, the early knife was designed with a long, sharply pointed blade and short handle—the dagger.

A PAIR OF KNIVES

During the 14th century a knife designed solely for the purpose of eating begins to appear at the table. For the wealthy this developed into a pair of knives, one to hold the meat with and the other to cut up and eat it. The knife was the diner's personal property which he carried in a sheath attached to his belt. Women usually wore it attached to their chatelaine, which hung from the belt and carried a variety of small domestic gadgets such as important keys, scissors, and in later periods a watch.

This use of a pair of knives was the early beginnings of elegance at table and a concern for manners!

Knives were considered a much honoured gift. The Worshipful Company of Cutlers record a pair given to their Lord Mayor as early as 1468, and the custom continued until after the Restoration in 1660.

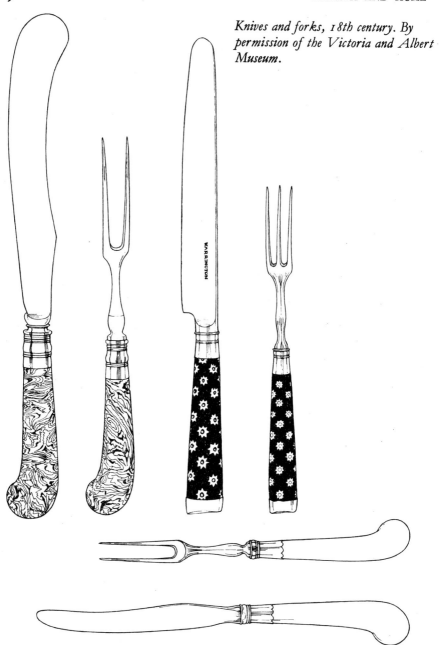

Knives and forks, 18th century. By permission of the Victoria and Albert Museum.

THE LENGTHENING BLADE

A change in design occurred in the 17th century when the knife blade lengthened to two almost parallel edges which ended in a point. About the middle of the same century the blade widened and the point was cut off to give a square tip. By the end of the century a curved blade became fashionable; this developed into the scimitar blade. This change in shape coincided with the appearance of the fork at the table. The diner need no longer spear his meat with his knife. Another step in the sophistication of table etiquette.

The scimitar-bladed knife was common throughout Europe in the 18th century, but by the end of the century the straight-bladed knife had begun to make its appearance.

MASS PRODUCTION

The 19th century saw the mass production of table knives, with designs being confined to a few standard shapes. The blade was of steel with handles of bone, horn, ebony, ivory, wood, silver, nickel silver alloy, silver plate and cheap celluloid, depending on what one could afford.

The shape was now fairly stereotyped with a long parallel blade and rounded tip, though some had a slightly upturned and tapered tip.

An important development, from the housewife's point of view, was the advent of the stainless steel blade during the 1920s. This saved hours of cleaning stained steel blades.

THE SHORTENED BLADE

An interesting change in design has been the modern knife with its shortened blade and longer handle. The thinking behind today's shortened blade is mainly economics; as only a small portion of a knife blade is used for cutting up food, why waste steel, an expensive commodity, on a longer blade?

Steak knives, usually with a serrated blade, are a post-Second World War addition to table cutlery.

The advent of the dishwasher has brought about the manufacture of knives with blade and handle moulded in one piece of stainless steel.

THE SPOON

The spoon also reflects changing fashions. The spoon of the Middle Ages had a rounded bowl for scooping up and eating the pottages and 'messes' of that period. (Messes were generally dishes of meat which had been pounded with a pestle and mortar to a paste-like consistency). The handles were short and sturdy so they could be stowed away in a pocket after use, as everybody carried his own knife and spoon with him.

Spoons were of wood, horn, bone, and towards the end of the period, of pewter. Silver spoons didn't appear at the dinner table until the 13th century, and then only for the wealthy.

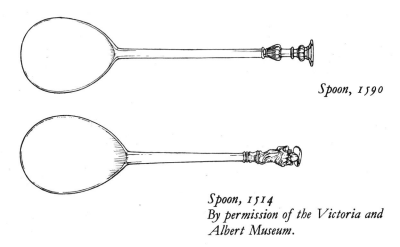

Spoon, 1590

Spoon, 1514
By permission of the Victoria and Albert Museum.

CHANGE OF SHAPE

By the end of the Renaissance the spoon had evolved into an oval bowl which could be used for soups and liquids. And at the end of the 16th century this shape had further developed into a flat oval-shaped bowl with a long, slim handle to cope with the fashion for stiffly starched ruffs.

CHANGE OF MATERIALS

The changes in materials used for cutlery coincided with those taking place in other table appointments.

The use of the pewter spoon was the accepted fashion for all but the rich, until the discovery of Britannia metal in about 1769. The Sheffield City Museum has moulds for casting pewter rat-tail pattern spoons dated 1680.

Britannia metal was an improvement on pewter in that it was much harder and took a good polish, and by 1809 Britannia metal spoons were being sold for as little as 4s. 3d. per dozen. (In modern terms this is less than 25p, but one has to remember that it could be a week's wage for, say, a farm labourer of that time).

The next development in low-priced cutlery came with the introduction of EPNS in the 19th century (see page 93) and then stainless steel in the 20th century.

Dessert or pudding spoons were not in common use during the 18th and 19th centuries. The two main sizes were the tablespoon and the teaspoon.

Wealthy households in the 19th century would order sets of silver cutlery to suit their particular requirements. In fact, during the pretentious Victorian and Edwardian eras there was such a plethora of cutlery on the table at the same time that it was often difficult to know the use of each piece.

BASIC SHAPE

The spoon hasn't really changed its basic shape since the long handle was introduced to overcome the difficulty of eating in a high ruff, though the bowl may have changed slightly to accommodate the whim of a designer.

THE FORK

The fork, except for a two-pronged affair used by the carver in the Middle Ages, and the sweetmeat fork, wasn't seen at the table in England until about the mid-16th century. Although it had been introduced from the Continent at the beginning of the 16th century, it hadn't caught on. The fork did not take precedence over one of the pair of knives at the well-appointed table until a hundred years after its introduction.

The design of the fork was continually changing. It started as a two-pronged implement made in silver, and was completely straight and flat. It next developed three and then four prongs or tines. It also began to follow the style of the spoon, and so the three-piece set of knife, fork and spoon began to evolve. The 'set' was usually carried in a special case.

THE SET

By the beginning of the Georgian era it was becoming fashionable in wealthy households to lay the table with the knife, fork and spoon by the plate—much as we do today. Diners were now no longer expected to supply their own cutlery when asked out to dinner, though special travelling sets were still the custom for use at inns and hostelries where cutlery was not generally supplied with the meal.

CHEAPER METALS

Although forks were, in general, made of silver, some low-priced steel and iron forks were produced in the 18th and early 19th century. Pewter and Britannia metal were both too soft for the satisfactory manufacture of forks.

It wasn't until the discovery of EPNS in the 19th century, the development of mass production as a result of the industrial revolution, and the rise in the standard of living that forks came into general use.

It is in fact only some 120 years since the knife, fork and spoon were in daily use on the table of all types of households, both rich and poor.

A small sweetmeat fork had been in use since the 11th century for picking up such delicacies as sweetmeats and fruit.

DESSERT AND FISH SETS

During the early 18th century the French introduced a knife specially designed for peeling and cutting fruit with a blade of gold or silver, as steel stained easily. It was an easy development for the sweetmeat fork to become the dessert fork and to join the smaller dessert knife, so making a dessert knife and fork.

The habit of laying a special dessert knife and fork for fruit continued until the Second World War, but with the advent of stainless steel cutlery and the lack of servants this custom died out in most households.

The fashion for fish knives and forks, which were usually more elaborately decorated and shaped for identification, began to disappear with the arrival of stainless steel, as this material, unlike silver, doesn't retain the flavour of fish.

DESIGN AND CUSTOMS

Eating customs become more and more international, and this affects design today. For example, the American fashion of cutting up food with a knife and then eating it with the fork alone has brought about a change in design—a fork with short prongs and a deeper, slightly hollow base. The short prongs give strength for breaking up vegetables, etc., and the deeper, hollow base acts as a scoop.

Another development is the less formal table-setting which mirrors today's trends in labour-saving devices. Whereas the Victorians and Edwardians were inordinately proud of their magnificent canteens of cutlery, we would look at them with the eye of a time and motion study expert counting the hours spent in care and maintenance.

FURTHER READING

The Story of Cutlery. J. B. Hamsworth. Benn Brothers, 1953.

Dinner is Served. Gerard Brett. Rupert Hart-Davis, 1968.

English Cutlery. 16th to 18th Century. J. F. Hayward. HMSO, 1957. (A Victoria and Albert Museum booklet.)

Tableware. Elizabeth Good. Council of Industrial Design. Macdonald, 1969.

Kitchen and Table. Colin Clair. Abelard-Schuman, 1964.

A History of Domestic Manners and Sentiments during the Middle Ages. Thomas Wright. Chapman & Hall, 1862. (This is a fascinating book full of delightful drawings and engravings. I obtained a copy from my local public library.)

Made in Sheffield. (Some notes on the manufacture of cutlery.) Issued by the Sheffield Cutlery Manufacturers' Association, Light Trades House, Melbourne Avenue, Sheffield LO.

Antique Drinking Glasses. A pictorial history of glass drinking vessels by Albert Hartshorne. Brussel & Brussel, New York, 1968.

Glass through the ages. E. Barrington Haynes. Penguin Books, 1948.

Making Glass. Glass Manufacturers' Federation, 19 Portland Place, London, W.1.

Treen and Other Wooden Bygones. Edward H. Pinto. G. Bell & Sons, 1969.

Movable Feasts. Arnold Palmer. OUP, 1953.

A Glimpse of Old Table Settings based on notes by Kate Doggett, *Antiques,* September 1934. (This article has some excellent illustrations of various table settings through the ages.)

4 Ice Cold

PERISHABLE FOODS

The satisfactory preservation and storage of perishable foodstuffs has been a constant problem to man. The ancient Greeks extended the life expectancy of fresh foods by storing them in earthenware dishes immersed in very cold water—a practice still in use in certain areas of the world today. Salting, pickling, smoking and sun-drying of foods were practical methods of preserving food, though not necessarily producing the most palatable result. These methods are still practised today but under controlled conditions.

ICE-HOUSES

Ice and snow have been used for cooling drink and food since earliest times. Ice-houses were very common in this country in the 17th century, and in some country homes now owned by the National Trust you can see very fine examples. Nearly all of them are still in working order.

These ice-houses were built on the principle of good insulation, with a low compartment where a mixture of snow and salt could be shovelled at appropriate times during the winter months. Vents opened to the north-east wind, so that a circular section of thick ice could be formed, the surface of which was then covered with straw. In one or two cases the ice-house was built close to a stream, which was diverted during the winter months and allowed to turn to ice inside the building.

These ice-houses supplied large quantities of ice required for preserving and cooking purposes.

IMPORTED ICE

At the turn of the century the import of ice grew to about 500,000 tons, most of which went to the towns and some to country homes where it was used for ice safes. The ice was brought by boat from Norway, or by fast clipper from America.

Some British farmers deliberately flooded their lands in the winter to produce ice for domestic use.

ICE CHESTS

Until the advent in this country during the 1920s of the mechanical domestic refrigerator, the British housewife had to depend on ice-houses and ice chests (or boxes or refrigerators as they were called). They were cupboards or chests lined with zinc and insulated with felt, asbestos, or slag wool; the ice had to be placed in a well-insulated compartment to keep it cool.

ARTIFICIAL COLD

The Venetians, during the 16th century, found that a mixture of one-third salt and two-thirds snow would induce a temperature cold enough to freeze water.

There were many attempts to discover a way of making low temperatures artificially. Among those who achieved practical results was William Cullen, a Scottish physician who, in 1755, experimenting with the vacuum principle, demonstrated a means of evaporating water by using an air pump and obtained temperatures sufficiently low to make ice. And in 1810, Sir John Leslie, another Scotsman, improved upon William Cullen's method by introducing a saucer of sulphuric acid to help absorb the water vapour.

The man to get nearest to the hub of the problem was Jacob Perkins, an American engineer living in London, who produced the first vapour compressor unit using a fluid which evaporated quickly. He was granted a patent in 1834 and his machines were used in breweries and meat-packing plants.

A 19th-century refrigerator. By permission of the Radio Times Hulton Picture Library.

CE SAFES.

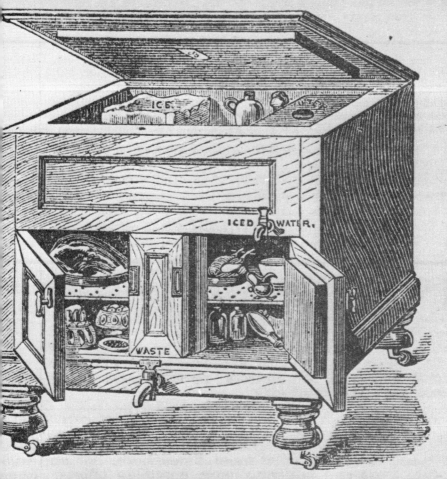

The **NEW DUPLEX REFRIGERATOR.**
gistered. For Wenham Lake or Rough Ice. PRIZE
DAL REFRIGERATORS. Fitted with Water Tanks
l Filters. The New American DOUBLE-WALL ICE
ATER PITCHER. Suitable for Wine Cup, &c. The
erican BUTTER DISH, with revolving lid, for use with
. WENHAM LAKE ICE delivered in town for less
n 1d. per lb., or forwarded into the country, in packages
s. 6d., 4s., 8s., and upwards, by "GOODS TRAIN," without
ceptible waste. Illustrated Price Lists free on applica-
n.

ENHAM LAKE ICE COMPANY
125. STRAND. LONDON Corner of Savoy-street).

On the continent, Ferdinard Carré, a Frenchman, utilised ammonia gas as a refrigerant and in 1859 he developed an ammonia absorption machine.

MECHANICAL REFRIGERATORS

The two types of refrigerators in use today are the compressor type and the absorption type.

In the compressor type the vapour is compressed and changes back into liquid when passed through a condenser. The electric motor and compressor are sealed in one unit and need no attention.

The absorption type is silent and has no moving parts and is operated by the external application of a small amount of heat, a small gas flame or electrical element, to a refrigerant.

COMMERCIAL REFRIGERATION PLANTS

In 1876, Jacob Perkins' apparatus was further developed by a German professor of thermodynamics, Carl von Linde. Linde introduced ammonia into the vapour-compression system of refrigeration. This is the basis of the majority of refrigeration plants in use today. The first applications of the artificial production of cold were used in cargo ships which carried perishable foods, such as meat, from abroad.

DOMESTIC MODELS

Domestic refrigeration had its origins in America, where the long hot summers made the housewife very dependent on ice for the preservation of foods as well as for cooking. There was a need to produce a practical and commercially viable domestic refrigerator, so much so that by 1880 nearly 3,000 patents had been taken out in America for various ideas on refrigeration.

The first electric domestic refrigerator was developed in a back yard wash-house in Indiana. In 1919, some forty domestic refrigerators had been built, and the Guardian Frigerator Company, later Frigidaire Corporation (Michigan) had been born. Frigidaire started manufacturing in Britain in 1923. The first refrigerator had been sold in Britain in 1921. It was a French compressor model and was bought by Lord Leconfield.

Research still continued and two young Swedish students, von Platen and Munters, succeeded in developing a continuous absorption unit during the early 1920s. Their idea was acquired and further developed industrially. Four years later, 1926, a Swedish made water-cooled absorption model was marketed in Britain. It was 10 cu ft capacity and housed in a wooden cabinet. It cost £48.50, a price which at that time would only be paid by the well-off.

In 1927 absorption type refrigerators were being manufactured in Britain for the first time, at Luton. Previously they had been imported. These refrigerators had wooden cabinets which were insulated with cork and lined with painted sheet metal. They were cooled by a continuous flow of cold water. The water-cooling method continued until 1930, but the wooden cabinets were soon superseded by steel cabinets. And by 1932 a freestanding, 1 cu ft model had been made and was selling at £19.50 a fairly popular price.

A product can only develop its full potential if the public can be persuaded to buy it in quantity. Two occurrences helped to popularise the use of early refrigerators. The introduction of the Food Preservation Act in 1926 which forbade the use of certain chemical preservatives; and the manufacture of small gas-operated refrigerators which could be produced at a low price.

POPULARITY

The 1939–45 war brought to a halt the manufacture of domestic refrigerators, but near the end of the war the British Government, realising that there would be a chronic shortage of houses, began the design of thousands of temporary pre-fabricated houses. The kitchens were tiny, but to overcome the obvious problems of food storage, each 'pre-fab' had a built-in refrigerator. Until this time refrigerators had been considered a privilege of the rich; now a much wider public could see how useful they were and how they reduced waste.

In 1960, 22 per cent of British homes had refrigerators. By 1969, this had risen to 56 per cent.

RECENT DEVELOPMENTS

Basically the refrigerator hasn't changed. It has become more sophisticated with the innovation of the 'star' rating system of the frozen food compartments, which allows the housewife to plan her purchase and use of frozen foods more efficiently; the development of the push-button defrosting cycle; improved methods of insulation by the use of expanded plastics which take up less space than the old cork insulation and allow them to hold more food without increasing the size of the cabinet.

HOME FREEZERS

Freezing as opposed to the refrigeration of foodstuffs started with the growing meat industries of South America and New Zealand, when refrigeration plants were used for freezing the entire holds of ocean-going ships.

The home freezer is a miniature version of this commercial freezing machinery. The 'Deep Freeze' which is the trade name of an American company, became popular in America in the early 1950s. It was possible to hire space in a local 'deep freeze' which was owned by a butcher or some other private company. The housewife soon appreciated the convenience of a 'deep freeze' and began to demand a domestic model. Initially, no doubt, she compromised by installing a secondhand commercial ice-cream cabinet in her home. The development of out-of-town shopping centres, entailing journeys of up to thirty miles, also helped to make the freezer an essential piece of domestic equipment in America.

IN BRITAIN

Around the early 1960s the idea began to catch on in Britain. 29,000 units were sold in 1965 and in 1971 some 350,000 units. There are now probably almost one million home freezers in use in this country today.

A refrigerator of the 1930s—the advertiser's message determinedly linking it to 'gracious living'. By permission of the Electrical Development Association.

The basic design of the freezer hasn't changed, but various features have been added such as a pilot warning light to show that the temperature has risen inside, and a 'fast freeze' switch for bringing down the temperature quickly for fast freezing.

A British Standard for home freezers has been prepared which will incorporate a test to check the daily freezing capacity. This will ensure that the weight of fresh food inserted daily can be fast frozen without lowering the quality of food already frozen. The manufacturer will be required to state the amount of fresh food which can be frozen in 24 hours.

TYPES OF FREEZERS

There are three types of home freezers:

Chest freezers have a top opening lid. They hold the cold well; as cold air is heavier than warm air there is only a very slight loss of cold air when the freezer is opened.

Some models are rather deep, so it is not always easy to find a particular packet without disturbing much of the contents. Removable baskets or trays are recommended for holding the same type of foods which allow for ease in stacking and in selecting the food. Some cabinets are fitted with compartments.

Chest freezers only require defrosting once or twice a year.

Vertical or upright freezers have front opening doors rather like ordinary refrigerators. Some models have inner doors or drawers which help to prevent loss of cold air. They are compact and take up less floor space, fitting well into a planned kitchen unit.

They are easy to pack and unpack and stocks can be quickly checked. Fittings include shelves and/or baskets.

There is little difference in electricity consumption between the two shapes, but upright freezers need rather more frequent defrosting.

REFRIGERATOR/FREEZER

Some refrigerators, usually the larger and more expensive models, include a separate freezing compartment, which is capable of freezing small quantities of fresh produce as well as giving long-term storage of commercially frozen foodstuffs. One compartment is a conventional refrigerator and the freezing unit is above it, with a separate door.

FURTHER READING

'A to Zero of Refrigeration'. General Motors. Michigan, USA.

'Food Freezing at Home'. Gwen Conacher. The Electricity Council.

Kitchen and Table. Colin Clair. Abelard-Schuman, 1964.

'Home Preservation of Fruit and Vegetables'. Bulletin 21. HMSO, 1968.

'The Economics of Freezing'. Rosemary McRobert. *Home Economics,* March, 1972.

The History of Technology. Ed. Charles Singer, E. J. Holmyard, A. R.Hall, Trevor I. Williams (Vol. V, 1850–1900). Oxford at the Clarendon Press.

Dictionary of Inventions and Discoveries. Ed. E. F. Carter. Frederick Muller, 1966.

5 Dishwashers

'Doing the washing-up' has a special place in the history of Women's Lib. Long before that phrase was coined, women were objecting to being 'chained to the kitchen sink'; and when men, married to wage-earning wives, began to help in the home, washing-up was one of the first tasks they undertook. Is the subsequent rise of the dishwasher a coincidence? Be that as it may, perhaps dishwashers merit a very short chapter to themselves.

AMERICAN DEVELOPMENT

It is estimated that only some 200,000 dishwasher units were in use in Britain in 1971, yet the first step towards the developnent of an automatic mechanical dishwashing machine came about as early as 1850 when Z. Houghton of Ogden, New York, took out a patent for a crude appliance with a paddle wheel that splashed water over the dishes. After this first effort there were a number of attempts to pioneer a practical and efficient dishwasher. Most of the early models were extremely primitive and unwieldy, some requiring as many as fourteen different manual operations. For instance, the washing water had to be heated on a range; the machine was then filled with the hot water by a bucket or a jug; the soap, probably home-made, was chopped or shaved into small particles and added to the dishwasher machine; and after each washing operation the water had to be drained off into a bucket which was then emptied. These machines could hardly be called labour-saving.

In 1865 a patent was issued for a machine with a propeller set in a cylindrical tank. This was the first time a propeller was used to move or agitate the water. In the model the dirty plates were set in a rack over the propeller, which, when turned by a handle, splashed soapy water over the dishes. The use of a propeller and a plate rack are both principles used in modern dishwashers.

By 1900 more than thirty patents had been taken out. However, the first really effective model was developed by two brothers, Willard and Forest Walker of Syracuse, New York, in 1909. The water in this machine was circulated by a system of plungers which forced the water from the bottom of the machine up and over the dishes. The Walker brothers next step forward was to produce a dishwasher driven by a petrol engine. I can't think that any housewife would appreciate a combustion engine in her kitchen! In 1914 the Walkers introduced a dishwasher powered by an electric motor. This machine was awkward and clumsy and many of the operations were still manual, as the electric motor was used only to drive the water over the dirty dishes.

Slowly dishwashers became more sophisticated. By 1919 a hose was being used to fill the machine, and a valve on the outside indicated the water level inside the tub. There were about twenty-seven makes of dishwashers on the American market by the end of the 1914–18 war.

Between the 1920s and the 1940s many improvements were made both in design and efficiency of performance. For instance, a 1928 model used an impeller (a disc-like propeller) for washing and rinsing the dishes; a front opening door was introduced, as prior to this machines had been top-opening only; dishwashers were now being permanently plumbed-in or were available as free-standing units.

From 1950 onwards dishwashers have become increasingly automatic, with operating programmes increasing in number and flexibility.

EUROPE AND BRITAIN

The dishwasher did not really appear in any quantity in Britain or on the Continent until the late 1950s, although some households had installed imported American models before this date.

TYPES OF DISHWASHERS

The basic concept of a dishwasher is an electrically driven pump to provide the power to produce the powerful jets of water needed for cleaning and rinsing the dirty dishes, and a drain pump.

There are various models which are designed to either stand on the floor, on a draining board, to be fixed to a wall, or built in below a draining board.

Different models offer a variety of programmes, but basically the cycles include the *heating cycle* in which the water is heated to the required temperature, the *washing cycle*, the *rinsing cycles* in which the dishes are rinsed at least twice, and finally the *drying cycle*. Some models include a prewash rinsing cycle where the dishes are rinsed only to hold them for washing at a later time. This is particularly useful in a small family when the machine may not be fully loaded after one meal, say, breakfast. A recent addition has been a pre-soak cycle when a biological wash powder* is used in a heated pre-wash cycle for heavily stained dishes, eliminating the need to hand-wash badly stained casserole dishes.

Programmes designed to deal with heavy or light soiling and for specific kitchen utensils have been recently introduced on some machines. A 'long' programme is suitable for washing saucepans, particularly those with a PTFE coating, oven-to-table ware and heavily stained dishes. This programme includes a prewash, a main wash, three cold rinses and one hot, and steam sterilisation. One manufacturer has produced a special saucepan programme which subjects pans to a greater pressure from rotating water jets at the base of the machine.

---

* Biological wash powders contain certain enzymes which are added to the normal detergent ingredients. These enzymes react on protein, such as egg—usually one of the hardest things to get rid of in dishwashing. These powders are also used in laundry-work.

Enzymes are complex organic molecules produced by living cells, but they are not alive themselves. Examples of enzymic reactions can be seen in bread and cheese making, and in fermenting wine and beer.

6 Twigs to Vacuums

THE FLOOR

To appreciate the development of household floor cleaning equipment it is helpful to take a brief look at the history of floor coverings.

During the Middle Ages the floors of castles, manor houses, town houses and large farmhouses were generally of stone, slate or oak boards with rushes laid on top for warmth and quiet. By the 17th century the rushes had probably given way to woven rush matting. Oriental carpets were imported but were usually used as tablecovers, although the wealthy put them on the floors of their private apartments.

Carpets were being woven at Wilton and Axminster by the middle of the 18th century. They were expensive and could only be afforded by the rich.

Until the 19th century the floors of the downstairs rooms of the majority of cottages were made of bare earth beaten down to give a hard surface; the sleeping area under the roof had a rough wooden floor.

Linoleum was the first reasonably priced, mass-produced floor covering. It made its appearance in 1860 when F. Walton discovered that a mixture of oxidised linseed oil and ground cork, compressed and dried, made a useful floor covering.

The last twenty years have seen a wide range of floor coverings in use in the home, such as ceramic tiles, linoleum and cork, thermoplastic tiles and sheets such as vinyl, PVC; cement such as concrete and terrazzo; rubber flooring and many forms of carpeting.

A revolution in carpeting came with the introduction in the 1950s from America of tufted carpets which brought the price of wall-to-wall carpeting within the reach of most families. The economical price is due to the fact that the manufacturing process of 'tufting' is quicker than traditional weaving. So popular is this carpeting that 81 million yards were produced in 1971 compared with 56 million yards of traditionally woven carpet. It is forecast that by 1980 some 176 million yards will be needed to supply the ever-demanding market. One reason for this popularity is the easy-care properties of the main materials, nylon staple and polyester fibre. These fabrics have a high degree of abrasion, dirt, fire and moisture resistance. They are, therefore, stain resistant because they are non-absorbent. But even so spillages should be removed immediately. Another advantage is that they are unattractive to moths.

EARLY BRUSH MAKING

The first floor cleaning tool was a broom or brush in some primitive form—probably prehistoric woman picked up a bundle of twigs or a tuft of rushes and swept out her cave. She may at some later date have bound the bundle to a piece of bone or branch of a tree to make a handle. It probably looked like a rather rough relative of the besom broom used today.

Brushes have been taken so much for granted that there is little documented history. They were known to the Greeks, Romans and ancient Egyptians.

Until the 1870s brushes were made by hand in ways which had not altered for centuries, and some 5 per cent of domestic brushes are still made by this method.

BRUSHMAKING BY HAND

The wood used for the stock or brush backs is seasoned in the brushmaker's yard for some twelve months or more. It is then cut into rough stocks which are mechanically sanded and the wood is sealed so that it will take a coat of lacquer.

The brush is now ready for filling. The definition of a brush filling is regulated by law, for instance, *bristle* refers *only* to the hair of hog, pig or boar; *hair* is of animal origin and must contain no vegetable or synthetic fibre, whalebone, or feather; *vegetable fibres* are also classified in detail.

HAND FILLING

There are two methods, 'pan-setting' and 'drawing', both of which have been used in some form or another for generations.

PAN-SETTING

The stock has holes bored in it at regular intervals, angled to give the best possible 'spread' of bristle, hair or fibre. The holes are bored only

Pansetting a hand-brush. By permission of Briton Chadwick.

part way through. The majority of this boring today is mechanical, though in the past it was done freehand, without any pattern to guide the brushmaker.

The stock is now ready for filling. The tufts or 'knots' of bristle, hair or fibre are selected by the panhand. He dips them in pitch, binds them with string or 'thrum', dips them in pitch again and sets them in the holes, giving each 'knot' a little twist which allows the hair to splay out, giving the finished brush a bushy effect or a good 'spread', the hallmark of a panset brush.

DRAWING

In this method the knots of filling are bound with wire which is drawn through the brush and secured at the back. Holes of two diameters are bored through the stock. The first hole which holds the hair or bristle is large; the small hole, which is a continuation of the large hole, takes the wire. The brushmaker passes the wire in a loop through the hole from the back of the brush, slips the knot of hair or bristle into the loop, pulls it through and fastens it.

Once the drawing is finished the back of the brush is then glued or screwed into position to hide the wire.

Whilst pansetting is more common this last method of brushmaking is still used today. If you can find an old worn-out brush, take off the back and admire the wiring.

BRUSHMAKING BY MACHINE

In the early 1870s a young American, E. F. Bradley, arrived in England with plans for making solid-back brushes by machinery.

His machine, though only capable of making simple brushes, could fasten more than one hundred knots a minute into a stock which had already been bored by machine.

Machine-made brushes had the advantage that they were cheap, well-made and of a uniform quality. There was no danger of the brushes splitting or

Machine filling in a brush factory.
By permission of Briton Chadwick.

coming to pieces and the knots were securely fastened by wire staples. The filling was doubled over a piece of wire which the machine then cut off and formed into a staple. In one movement the knot and wire staple were punched into the hole. When the knot reached the bottom of the hole the points of the wire staple entered the wood, anchoring the knot. This is still the base of modern machines. And at least 95 per cent of all domestic brushes are machine-made.

PLASTICS

The 1950s saw the use of plastic monofilaments and plastic stocks. The traditionalist says that natural fillings tend to be more efficient for scrubbing and paint brushes as they absorb and hold water more readily than synthetic materials. A synthetic floor brush is inclined to flick or attract dust rather than gather it together.

MOPS

The history of the mop is vague, but presumably there has been some form of mop since man covered his floors with tiles and mosaics.

The basic cotton mop which consists of a cluster of cotton fibres mounted on the end of a stock goes back some centuries in time. However, at the end of the 19th century a refined version of this type of mop was being made commercially in America for domestic use; it arrived on these shores in the early 20th century.

At the turn of the century parquet flooring became fashionable in the main rooms of large houses. Parquet should not be washed with water, so the impregnated cotton mop was introduced. This mop, impregnated with linseed oil or some floor polishing substance, absorbed surface dust and must have saved many hours of the housewife's time. Today it is impregnated with siliconised oil.

The next development came about due to changes in floor surfaces. Wall-to-wall carpeting became cheap and fashionable, as did thermoplastic sheets and tiles. Consequently, the 1950s saw the introduction of cellulose sponge mops. These absorb and hold water well and don't suffer from bacteriological decay. This ability to retain water is important as modern flooring can be damaged by excessive wetness.

In the mid-1950s a self-squeezing or lever-operated sponge mop with a cellulose head appeared on the market. This meant that the user's hands need never come in contact with the water and strong detergents. To date the principle of this mop has not changed, but the design has become more streamlined. Various click-on heads are available for the different cleaning jobs, such as a dry mop, floor polisher, liquid polish applicator, broom, scrubber, carpet shampoo brush.

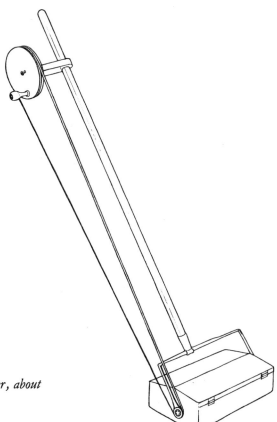

A 'Prestige' carpet sweeper, about 1898.

CARPET SWEEPERS

The first workable domestic rotary carpet sweeper was developed and made by Mr. M. R. Bissell of Grand Rapids, Michigan, USA, in 1876 although patents had been taken out as early as 1825 for a road cleaning machine to which brooms mounted on a shaft revolved like paddles of a water wheel. The Ewbank was introduced to the British housewife in the late 19th century.

These early models were heavy and clumsy by comparison with today's streamlined models, but the fundamental design has not changed. Today's models are lighter and slimmer and designed to go easily under low modern furniture. The casing material is now of high quality hardboard or steel with a synthetic trim.

Recently a dual purpose model was introduced with a two-position control dial which enables the sweeper to be used on all kinds of floor surfaces—carpets, linoleum, parquet or tiles. The dustpans and the brush are lowered by switching the dial to sweep hard floors. There is also an up-to-the-wall model with angled brushes to sweep close to the skirting board.

CARPET SHAMPOOERS

1959 was the year the upright hand-operated carpet shampooer was introduced to the British market, although it had been in use in America for some years. This allows the housewife to 'shampoo' her carpets quickly and efficiently. The principle hasn't changed since 1959. The designs of appliances and shampoo have become more sophisticated.

Some electrical polishers will cope with shampooing carpets. Different brushes or pads are fitted into the foot of the machine for the job on hand. A foam sprayer attachment which will spray light-volume liquids like carpet shampoo and upholstery cleaners is available with some vacuum cleaners.

ELECTRIC FLOOR POLISHERS

These first appeared in Britain after the Second World War but the market is small, probably due to the increasing popularity of wall-to-wall carpeting.

VACUUM CLEANERS

The carpet sweeper was a step towards the invention of the vacuum cleaner. Another was the need in industry for the efficient removal and collection of dust and dirt, such as the dust from castings in iron foundries.

In the home the main methods of cleaning a carpet were to brush it with a stiff brush or carpet sweeper, or to take it outside and beat it in the open air. These methods were not really adequate. A carpet can hold its own weight in dirt and dust. Brushing and beating tends to make the dust fly around, landing on the poor unfortunate housewife and, of course, back onto the carpet itself again.

In 1860 a US patent was taken out covering a cleaner which consisted of a revolving brush combined with a current of air. The brush flicked up the dust which was then carried into the container by the current of air. The air came from bellows which were driven by a connecting rod attached to the wheels of the machine. This was the first type of vacuum cleaner in which the suction was constant. An added sophistication was an air-cleaning system. The dust-laden air was passed through water chambers which could be cleaned out and refilled. It must have been a heavy and clumsy piece of equipment to operate, and was probably only used in commercial carpet cleaning.

The next innovation was a machine driven by steam which beat the carpet with wooden flails—an idea based on the principle of the threshing machine. The machine was cumbersome and tended to be used by commercial operators who would come to a house, at the request of the housewife, removing the carpets for beating and then returning to relay them. When you think of the overcrowded rooms of Victorian households it must have been a mammoth operation to remove all the furniture and knick-knacks just to have your carpet beaten professionally!

About 1893 an Englishman, J. J. Harvey, took out a patent for a cleaner incorporating suction by hand-driven bellows with a surface dusting brush which could cope with books and pictures. No doubt the average housewife found a feather duster more manageable.

The transition from the large semi-portable machine to today's light, streamlined domestic vacuum cleaner took place between 1859 and 1910. The development during this period of the small electric motor and the provision of electric current in homes acted as a stimulant to the production of domestic appliances.

PUFFING BILLY

In 1901 a young British engineer, H. Cecil Booth, was invited to watch a cleaning demonstration of train carriages by a new 'dust machine' at St. Pancras Station, London.

It worked on the principle of a jet of air blowing dust and dirt from one end of the carriage into a container at the other end. The demonstration was not a complete success. However, it set Cecil Booth thinking and the story goes that when he got home he put a piece of wet cloth on a chair seat and sucked, reversing the process he had just witnessed at St. Pancras Station. Where he sucked there was a ring of dirt which gave him the idea of the vacuum cleaner.

Mr. Booth patented his invention in 1901 and the following year formed the Vacuum Cleaner Company Limited. Today the company is known as Goblin (B.V.C.) Ltd. Mr. Booth was also the originator of the phrase 'vacuum cleaner'.

The first vacuum cleaning machine was large, unwieldy and very expensive. The machine consisted of a powerful vacuum pump with a dust collecting filter. It was driven by a petrol or electric motor and was known as 'Puffing Billy'. Mounted on a horse-driven van it would be driven up to the house to be cleaned. Hoses would be put through a window of the house and the dust and dirt vacuumed off carpets, curtains and furniture.

Mr. Booth's invention was such a success that he was asked to clean the Coronation Carpet in Westminster Abbey for the coronation of Edward VII. The first two vacuum cleaners ever sold went to Buckingham Palace and Windsor Castle.

PORTABLE SUCTION CLEANERS

In 1904 Cecil Booth produced a completely portable hand-operated vacuum cleaner. Two people were needed to work this cleaner. One had to pump the bellows to create the suction and the other was required to manipulate the cleaning tool.

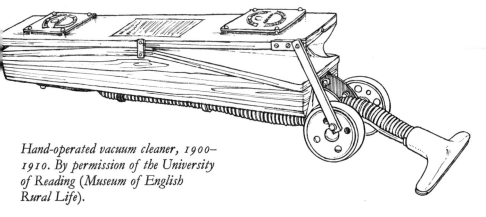

Hand-operated vacuum cleaner, 1900–1910. By permission of the University of Reading (Museum of English Rural Life).

The Cambridge and County Folk Museum has a heavy box-like vacuum cleaner on wheels with bellows attached on either side of the box to suck in the dust. Dated 1908, it was formerly used in Caius College, Cambridge.

ELECTRIC VACUUM CLEANERS

By 1914 electric vacuum cleaners were beginning to be manufactured and by 1917 they were in use in a number of households. Their introduction was slow, due mainly to the fact that servants were still plentiful, probably cheaper, more reliable and more efficient than these early machines.

The demand for vacuum cleaners grew. By 1930 some 300,000 machines were being sold each year, and by 1939 the figure had doubled to 600,000. The rapid growth was due, in part, to the fact that the hire purchase boom began in the 1930s and also due to domestic help becoming scarce.

AMERICAN UPRIGHT MODEL

While Cecil Booth was working away in Britain at perfecting his vacuum cleaner, Dr. William Noe of San Francisco developed a heavy portable machine with a motor-driven fan mounted on a wheeled chassis. In 1907 James M. Spangler applied for a patent for a portable electric machine. It had an electrically driven fan mounted vertically in a specially designed casing. Spangler's machine was incorporated into the Hoover model of 1908 and this was the beginning of the trend towards the *modern upright model.*

Meanwhile W. H. Hoover was introducing his first vacuum cleaner in 1907. It worked on the principle of suction plus the use of a revolving brush to loosen the dirt in the carpet. It was such a success that by 1917 a mail-order company in Chicago were advertising a portable machine which weighed only 12 lb and cost $19.45.

The same manufacturer, realising that a vibrating or agitating action would help to loosen and remove deeply embedded dirt, combined suction with a revolving brush in 1920. Six years later he further developed this principle with the addition of revolving metal bars which aided the revolving brush by gently beating the carpet on a cushion of air. These models were introduced into Britain in the mid-1920s.

This triple action has been the major change to the initial design presented in 1908.

Other improvements since the suction cleaner was first developed have been such additions as: air filters (introduced in 1926), the reduction of noise, automatic flex winders, cleaning heads which adjust automatically for carpets and hard floors, as well as a greater use of plastic and colour, and an increase in the versatility of tools supplied with the machine.

TYPES OF CLEANERS

There are three basic types of domestic vacuum cleaners available today: the upright, the cylinder and the sphere. About half the vacuum cleaners sold each year are the upright type, about a third are cylinder variety and the rest are the sphere and the smaller hand held cleaners.

The *upright* is generally considered to be the most suitable choice for fitted carpets. The modern upright is equipped with three or four adjustable positions for the brushes, allowing for efficient use on deep pile and shaggy weave carpets, medium pile, and low pile or cord carpets and felts. It is also possible to use this model on ordinary floor surfaces such as linoleum, tiles, etc.

Using the earliest of the Hoover cleaners in the decade before World War I.

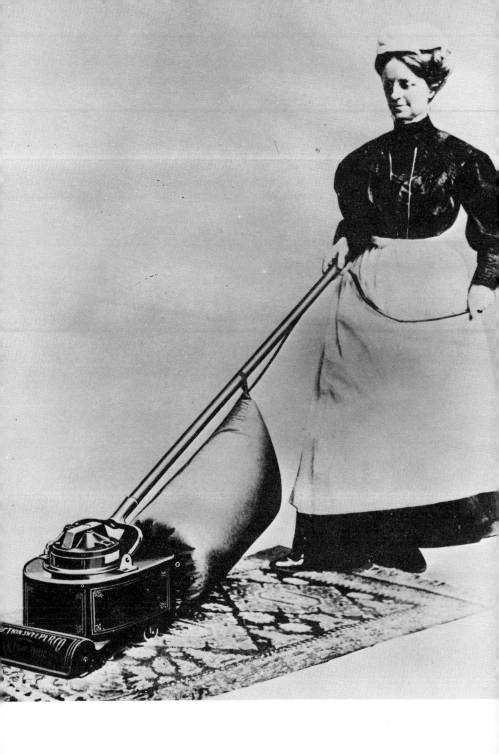

There are hand-held versions for cleaning inside a car, and for stairs, upholstery, curtains and chairs.

The *cylinder* type is a good choice if you have only a small area carpeted; it is easy to manoeuvre, especially on stairs, and is useful for cleaning smooth floor surfaces. Some models have brushes which adjust to the depth of the carpet.

FURTHER READING

All About Brushes. L. G. Shadbolt. Star Brush Co. Ltd. (no date).

In Love and Unity. A book about brushmaking. Tom Girton. Hutchinson, 1961.

Brushmaking Materials. F. Kidd. British Brush Manufacturers' Research Association, 1957.

The evolution of the Vacuum Cleaner. Design and Components in Engineering, April 15, 1970.

Clean Floors. Olwen Francis. Forbes Publications Ltd., 1971.

7 The Laundry

The luxury of personal washing and a regular change of clean clothes and household linen was the privilege of the well-to-do until around the 19th century. The wealthy had the time, the leisure, the advantage of personal servants to fetch and carry hot water for baths, and household servants to undertake the laundrywork.

Until the establishment of the cotton industry during the 18th century the poor, in general, dressed in tattered garments of rough hopsack, coarse wool, or leather, and they seldom wore any underclothes. Clothes were worn until they fell to pieces, as most of the fabrics would have shrunk beyond recognition, and soap was an expensive commodity. However, when the labourer's wife did any washing she would use wood ash mixed with animal fat, or a concoction known as 'lye' as a detergent. There were many different recipes for lye, which might have contained such ingredients as wood ash, hen dung and pigeon dung.

ELIZABETHAN WASHDAY

In Elizabethan times washday for the mass of people occurred so infrequently, about once every two or three months—probably less during winter—that it was heralded as a time for 'celebration'. A huge wooden tub was filled with dirty clothes and household linen and a lye water mixture was poured over, then all the available women and girls were pressed into service. They hitched up their dresses and stamped and danced on the wet clothes. The lye water was pressed out through a small hole in the base of the tub. More lye water was poured over the garments and the whole process repeated until the laundry was reasonably clean. It was then rinsed and spread out on the ground to dry.

A 19th CENTURY WASHDAY

Wash day became more frequent as cotton goods became cheaper and popular. Even so it was a laborious and long-drawn-out job.

An article published in the *Magazine of Domestic Economy* of February 1841 gave the following advice to a young housewife of modest means who was only able to afford one servant:

'The washing is performed at intervals of five, or should the weather be unfavourable, sometimes extended to six or seven weeks; and the practice is to commence, not like most persons do at the *beginning*, but at the *end* of the week.

'During Friday, the body linen and other fine things are *firsted, seconded*, and got ready for boiling on Saturday morning, when the servant should be up and at work by three o'clock. The boilings are performed in succession to the washing processes so as to get as much as possible done by Saturday evening, when a great portion is rinsed ready for hanging out, or may be allowed to remain in clear water.'

Here the writer tells us that the reason for starting on Friday is to give the servant Sunday off so that she can return on Monday morning at three o'clock 'with renewed strength'!

The advice continues: 'If all goes well, everything is finished, so far as regards washing, on Monday evening; should the weather prove unfavourable, the shirts, and other articles to be starched, are dried on Monday within doors on horses. Tuesday, after breakfast, starching commences, and the things are folded for mangling. On Wednesday the ironing begins with the shirts; all articles intended for mangling being now delivered out for that purpose, and required to be returned early in the afternoon, and allowed to remain all night. On Thursday the ironing is finished, generally by four o'clock, and the whole wash being accomplished, the various articles are reckoned over and put away.'

Public washing grounds, 1582
(Harleian MS). By permission of the
Radio Times Hulton Picture Library.

The writer comments that if the laundry had been sent out for washing it would have cost between £25 and £30 per annum but undertaken at home 'does not exceed (every expense included) five pounds'.

THE WASHING MACHINE

The early housewife discovered that lye water, or wood ash, or soap and water did not get clothes really clean. Some form of agitation or mechanical action was necessary to help loosen the grime and remove it from the garments. A large part of the world's women still wash their clothes and household linen by hand, squeezing, kneading, rubbing or beating them on flat stones or on a wooden washboard to release the grime.

The concept of today's washing machine was born as early as 1691 when John Tyzack, a Wapping glassmaker, took out letters patent for a machine which would oil and dress leather and cloth, wash clothes, mill sugar canes as well as pound seeds, charcoal and rags for papermaking. Unfortunately, Mr. Tyzack failed to realise his patent or to supply drawings.

The next attempt at producing a mechanical washing machine came in 1780 when a patent was issued to John Rogerson of Warrington. His machine could wash 'all sorts of household linen and wearing apparel', it also had a device for pressing out the water from the wet clothes, as well as a press for pressing gathers and pleats.

In 1782 Henry Sidgier introduced a machine which was the first piece of mechanical laundry equipment to use the rotary principle on which most modern machines are based. A cylindrical drum, turned by a handle, revolved in an outer case which held the washing water.

So the struggle went on to find a practical domestic washing machine.

In 1863 E. H. Smith submitted a patent for a reversible-action washing machine, which was an indication that washing machine inventors realised that a simple rotary action only resulted in a knot of tangled clothes.

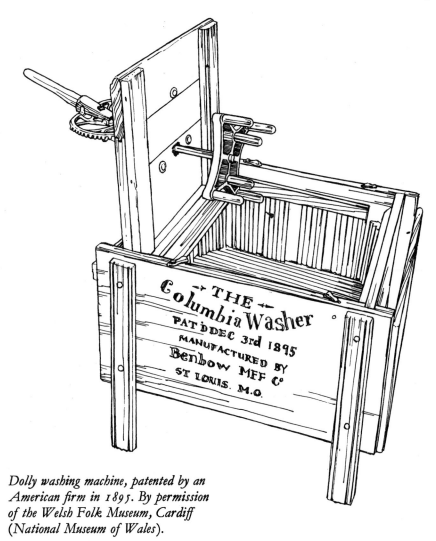

*Dolly washing machine, patented by an
American firm in 1895. By permission
of the Welsh Folk Museum, Cardiff
(National Museum of Wales).*

The design of many of these early machines was based on the washing movement of the hand, such as rubbing, squeezing, kneading and beating.

POSSER AND DOLLY STICK

The next development was the posser or dolly stick which copied the dunking up and down movement made by hand washing.

The posser or vacuum clothes washer had a cone-shaped copper head set on a long handle. The base was curved with holes in it. The dolly stick had many variations, from a simple wooden stick which was cone-shaped at one end to a three-legged milk stool mounted on a long handle. The principle of these washing aids was that, when they were pounded up and down on the washing, soapy water was forced through the clothes. In 1925 they were still in use.

Probably one of the most commercially successful machines was one first manufactured in the 1870s which worked on a revolving tub principle. Part of the instructions state: 'Always take care to turn the machine the right way so that the clothes are thrown off the underside of the "Midfeather", or inclined board, by which they receive both a rub and a dash at each turn.' The old handwashing principles are at work again.

The Martineau & Smith's *Hardware Trade Diary and Cash Book* for 1881 advertised a washer in which 'The clothes are passed between corrugated rollers which produces much the same effect as the knuckles in handwashing.'

THE ELECTRIC WASHING MACHINE

The majority of these early washing machines merely sloshed the clothes through soapy water. A major breakthrough came in April 1908 when an American, A. J. Fisher, attached a small electric motor to a washing machine. This motor drove a belt which caused a milk stool dolly, attached to the lid of the washing machine, to move backwards and forwards. This movement stirred up the surface of the water and agitated any clothes which happened to come in contact with the milking stool dolly's legs.

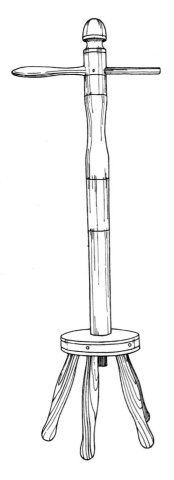

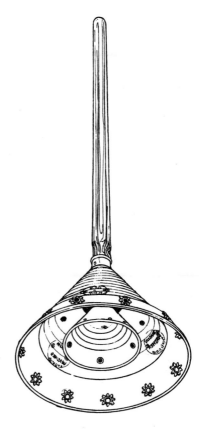

Two types of dolly, late 18th, early 19th century. By permission of the University of Reading (Museum of English Rural Life).

In 1922 an American firm put the milk stool dolly upside down into the bottom of the washing machine, causing the clothes (rather than the water) to be pushed to and fro, which more effectively removed the dirt.

FINS OR PADDLES

The next step was to replace the milk stool dolly with fins or paddles; the concept of the modern agitator machine.

BRITISH MACHINES

Electric washing machines were introduced into Britain in about 1917. In 1920 there were two types to choose from: the slow reversing cylinder model, and the slow reversing milk stool dolly type; both these models had wooden tubs.

In 1923 metal-tub domestic washing machines were imported from USA into this country, and in 1934 there was patented a domestic electric machine with all the moving parts encased in a neat, white-enamelled cabinet.

CENTRIFUGE

In the early 1920s the principle of centrifugal force (see page 134) was applied to washing machines, and by the late 1930s more than 335,000 washing machines built on this method were sold in America.

POST-WAR BOOM

The Second World War brought all manufacture of non-essential domestic equipment to a standstill. Peace however brought a boom in washing machine sales, and the development which started this was the brain child of George Gibson, an American.

His machine, which used a high speed, disc-like impeller set in the side of the tub, made possible manufacture of inexpensive, efficient washing machines.

This model was launched in Britain in 1947 with such success that the demand exceeded supplies for at least five years. The first models were simple, single-tub machines with hand wringers. In about 1950 immersion heaters were incorporated and in 1953 a power-operated wringer was available.

A washing machine of 1920, with attached wringer. By permission of Radiation Ltd.

TWIN-TUB

Although the power-driven wringer was efficient, a lot of water was left in the clothes, and most housewives still found drying a problem. This problem was solved with the launching of a twin-tub machine in 1957. This compact design combined an impeller washing machine and a spinner side by side in the same casing.

AUTOMATIC MACHINES

In the 1950s there was only one automatic machine on the market. It was a small rotary drum machine which washed, rinsed and spun, requiring the user only to load and push the 'on' button. However, in 1961 there appeared a machine which was programmed by a keyplate to produce a full wash, rinse and spin cycle automatically.

The fully automatic machine has become progressively more sophisticated, with some models including three full, biological wash programmes (for biological wash, see footnote, page 108); while other machines include a prewash cycle for extra dirty clothes, and one model automatically carries on with the wash programme after the pre-wash.

Most automatics relate their wash programme to the garment labels of the Home Laundering Consultative Council.* These list eight wash programmes to suit the fabric, and details are given in the washing machine instruction leaflets.

In 1971 there was a choice of twenty-six single-tub automatic washing machines, eighteen twin-tubs, and a small assortment of non-automatic single-tubs, usually fitted with a power wringer.

---

* The Home Laundering Consultative Council was set up in 1961 from the major industries with an interest in the laundering and dry cleaning of garments and textiles.

1962 saw the introduction of standardised washing temperatures, and their descriptions for use in washing machines. 1963 brought about the standardisation of domestic iron settings in relation to fabrics. The HLCC's care labelling scheme was published in 1966, providing a standard form of advice on care of fabrics when washed or dry cleaned. It is now so familiar that we have not thought it necessary to reproduce it in this book.

Further information is available from the Home Laundering Consultative Council, 41/42 Dover Street, London W1X 4DS.

MECHANICAL AGITATION

There are three mechanical means, other than boiling, of moving or agitating water in a washing machine:

1. *The impeller or pulsator*—this is a wheel, housed in the side or bottom of the tub, which rotates in a clockwise direction.

2. *The agitator* has three or four fins or paddle-shaped blades attached to a spindle which is set in the centre of the tub. It rotates backwards and forwards in half turns, driving the clothes and the water vigorously together.

3. *Tumble action*—a horizontal drum rotates either in one, or in alternate directions, lifting the clothes up and allowing them to fall back through the water.

TYPES OF MACHINES

The three main types of washing machines available are:

Single-tub machines which consist of a tub containing the heater, the agitator and a wringer. The agitator can be either the impeller or pulsator type, or the agitator type with fins or paddle-shaped blades rotating backwards and forwards. Some models are unheated and rely on hot water from the tap. The wringer is fixed to the machine and can be hand or power operated.

Twin-tub machines are basically the single-tub machine mentioned above with a spindrier in the same casing. Some models are semi-automatic in that they contain thermostats and automatic wash cycles; automatic rinsing is available once the clothes have been transferred manually from the washing tub to the spindrier.

Automatic machines carry out a pre-selected programme of washing, rinsing and spindrying, once the controls have been set to the required sequence. For example, a complete automatic programme for heavy cotton fabrics may include a soak, pre-wash or biological wash, followed by a spin and rinse; a main wash; a number of spins and rinses, followed by a final spin.

Washing is usually by tumble action or by agitator action. Most tumble machines are front opening; agitator machines are top opening.

There is a drum automatic machine which carries out all the operations of an automatic machine. It tumble-dries the load as well, but is expensive.

SPIN DRIERS

As early as the 18th century, inventors were exploring a way of extracting water from fabric by mechanical means. Efficient methods of water extraction were required for the textile and dyeing industries as well as for laundrywork. In 1830 the principle of the centrifuge was discovered, and in the 1920s it was applied to an American washing machine.

In theory it is a cylindrical basket revolving at high speeds. The clothes or fabric are pressed against the side of the cylinder by centrifugal force, and the water is forced out of the material, passing through holes in the container, and then out through an outlet pipe into a drain or sink.

Rather surprisingly, it was not until 1956 that an electric spin drier appeared on the British market, to be followed by a gravity model in 1958.

TUMBLER DRIERS

These work on the same principles as a tumble washing machine. The drum revolves in one direction only and hot air is either drawn in or blown through the load. Tumbler driers were first introduced into this country from America in the early 1950s. The first British model was produced in 1951. However, tumbler driers didn't appear in any quantity in this country until about 1966.

WASH BOILERS

In hot countries where water distribution is primitive, women still do their washing outside by the bank of a river, at a well, or in stagnant pools. The British weather didn't allow the housewife to wash outside for more than a few months of the year. So perhaps we can thank the weather for the introduction of the wash boiler, usually set on a brick plinth with space underneath for a fire, in an out-house or lean-to. No doubt the housewife was quick to appreciate that boiling softens hard water and works as an agitator, helping to loosen the dirt in the clothes.

Modern wash boiler design began to develop with the introduction of gas in the 19th century. A gas-powered, compact, free-standing wash boiler was manufactured and marketed, in 1895, by William Henry Dean, the founder of W. H. Dean & Son Ltd. These early boilers were made in heavy, black cast iron.

The next step was galvanising, which was coating the iron with zinc as a protection against corrosion.

In 1918 the retail price of a galvanised gas heated wash boiler was £1 7s.; in 1928 it had risen to £2 7s. 6d. and by 1969 it was £9 18s. (£1.35, £2.37½, £9.90).

Wash boilers did not change their basic shape until the late 1930s, but enamel in the early 1930s was added as a choice of fabric.

1938 produced a thought for kitchen planning with the introduction of a neat electric sink model. This was square in shape and fitted alongside the sink (there were no built-in kitchen units at this period, remember). The boiler had adjustable legs so it could fit any height of sink, and the top, when closed, could be used as a draining board. The model fitted either the left or right-hand side of the sink. It had a three-heat regulator and was made in mottled enamel. The price was £6 16s. (£6.80).

In 1960 the same company was selling a compact, three-heat control electric wash boiler in all cream or all white enamelled casing, with a choice of coloured table top in turquoise or eau-de-Nil, for £12 12s. (£12.60).

Today, wash boilers are powered by either gas and/or electricity; the outer casing is enamel and designed to fit into a kitchen unit. The majority are supplied with a fold-away wringer. There is, however, still a demand for the cheaper, functional, galvanised type.

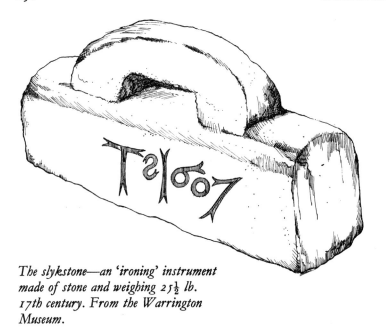

The slykstone—an 'ironing' instrument made of stone and weighing 25½ lb. 17th century. From the Warrington Museum.

IRONS

The ancient Egyptians, Chinese, Greeks and Romans used various implements for smoothing or pressing their clothes. The Romans, for instance, pressed their togas, while damp, with a wooden press called the prelum.

The Chinese are believed to have produced the first hand iron in a form we would recognise today. It was a small brass container fitted with a bone or wooden handle. The bottom of the container was filled with hot or burning coals.

IRONS IN BRITAIN

In Britain early ironing implements were probably fashioned from heavy, smooth stones and heated near an open hearth. This was a precarious business as the ironing stone could easily crack or explode with the heat.

A shaped, stone ironing implement was still in use in the 17th century and was known as a 'sleek', 'slick' or 'slykestone'. An example of a slykestone, which weighed 25½ lb, can be seen in the Warrington Museum, Lancashire. Slykestones were mainly used by tailors, as household articles were finished by being pressed in a large oak linen press. Clothes of this period were rarely washed, being made of silks, satins, velvets and taffetas.

Tailors in Elizabethan times used both slykestones and iron pressing equipment. The implement made from iron was known as a 'goose', because the handle was shaped like a goose's neck. The goose was long and narrow with a blunt end on which it stood before the open fire to heat. As it weighed anything from 8 to 30 lb it must have been very cumbersome to use and must have taken an exceptional time to heat up.

FASHION FOR RUFFS

The fashion for ruffs in the 16th century brought about the use of starch in laundrywork and consequently the goffering iron. The early starched ruff was set with a pair of wooden setting sticks.

The goffering iron was a round, slim, hollow iron barrel set on a tripod stand. The hollow barrel was heated by inserting a red hot bar of iron. The starched linen was then held in both hands and pulled taut over the hot barrel, making a series of crimps or frills.

BOX IRONS

Domestic irons came into gradual use during the 17th century. These were crude hollow boxes made of heavy cast iron with a lid, or a hinged door at the back. To heat them a red-hot lump of iron was thrust into the box by tongs.

In shape these irons resembled the type we use today. They had a rounded or a tapered front with a blunt rear. Most of these early irons had metal handles which even with a thick pad must have made them uncomfortably hot to use.

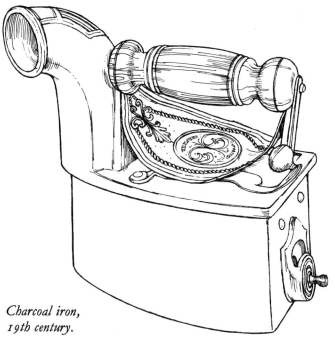

Charcoal iron,
19th century.

Box iron, 18/19th century.

By permission of the University of
Reading (Museum of English Rural
Life).

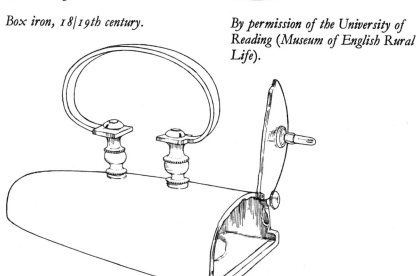

Another type of early box iron was a chimney or charcoal iron. Hot charcoal was inserted through a small hole in the back. The chimney was about 3 in high to allow fumes to escape; it also acted as a 'draw' to keep the charcoal glowing.

SAD IRONS

In 1738 Isaac Wilkinson of Cartmel took out a patent for 'a new sort of cast metallic box for smoothing linen'. This was the first iron to be cast from one solid piece of metal. Known as a flat iron it was often referred to as a 'sad' iron. 'Sad' is possibly derived from the Old English 'saed', meaning solid.

These early flat irons were heated by standing them on the blunt ends, near or against the coals. What hazards must have been involved in checking that the iron was not scorching hot, and cleaning and polishing the soleplate free of ash and coal dust? A trick used to give a smoother finish to the sole-plate was to 'slick' the flat iron with beeswax.

VICTORIAN ENGLAND

The development of the kitchen range in the 19th century helped to make ironing less arduous. The iron could now be heated on the hotplate on top of the range, or on a trivet hanging from a bar of the firebox, so that close contact with the soot and the ash of a naked fire was minimal. The soleplate still needed to be rubbed clean with a coarse cloth, removing any dust or fat which might have been on the hotplate.

The flat iron was still a hot and clumsy implement to use, and a laundry-maid must have been a skilled worker to cope with all the various fabrics, frills and flounces of Victorian fashion with an iron whose correct temperature was judged by instinct and years of practice. Think of testing the heat of an iron by holding it near your cheek or forearm, or by shaking a few drops of water and judging the heat of the iron by the strength of the hiss!

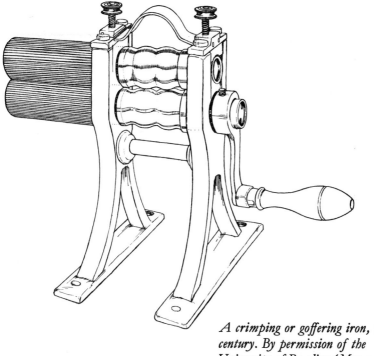

A crimping or goffering iron, 19th century. By permission of the University of Reading (Museum of English Rural Life).

WIDE CHOICE

By the mid-19th century the Victorian laundrymaid had a wide range of irons to choose from. The charcoal-heated box iron and the box iron heated with a slug of red-hot iron were still in use.

Flat irons were available in a variety of sizes and could vary from 4 to 10 in in length and from 2½ to 4½ in in width at the broad end.

A Victorian housewife using a heavy flat or 'sad' iron. It will be noted that she is ironing on a table—the ironing board does not yet seem to have made its appearance.

For coping with frills there was a crimping machine into which the trimming was inserted mangle fashion between two hollow rollers which were rotated by a handle. The machine was heated by inserting hot irons into the hollow rollers.

The Italian or Tally iron was advised for the pressing of flounces and crimping of frills. This was similar to the goffering iron.

A simple device for crimping frills was the crimping plate made of wood, usually elm. A grooved roller was cast backwards and forwards over damp starched frills laid on the plate.

There were also heavy glass 'calenders' shaped like a mushroom for smoothing and shining linen.

SELF-HEATING IRONS

The industrial revolution helped to bring about speedy improvements. There was a search for a self-heating iron in which the heating element was inside the iron, allowing the iron to be used continuously without having to wait for reheating. Charcoal, paraffin and methylated spirits were tried, but the true self-heating iron came about with the introduction of gas and electricity.

GAS IRONS

By the late 19th century a self-heating gas iron with a flexible tube was in use. Gas irons quickly gained popularity.

The basic shape of the iron didn't change. It could now be used almost on demand rather than waiting for a lump of metal to heat up.

A gas ironing set was advertised in 1927 as 'comprising two irons, heater and trivet'. The price of the set was £1 5s. (£1.25). Each iron weighed 5 lb. The irons were heated on a free-standing, compact gas burner. While one iron was in use the other was heating up.

In 1933 a self-heating gas iron with a flexible tube and detachable sole-plate, weighing 6¾ lb, was available in three finishes, the most expensive of which had all external parts nickel plated.

ELECTRIC IRONS

The electric iron was introduced into this country in the 1920s, although in the late 1890s the General Electric Company of America had made use of electricity in the home. The late arrival of electric irons was mainly due to the slowness of installing power.

The 1920 model was primitive by today's standards. The power supply was limited and subject to fluctuations, and there was no thermostatic heat control on the irons; so judging the heat of the iron relied, as in the past, on feel and practice. The iron had to be switched off and on to regulate the temperature. And due to dangers of overloading the supply the iron had to be sufficiently heavy to store enough heat to do an adequate job, without constant reheating. The average weight of these early irons was between 7 and 9 lb.

THERMOSTATS

The first thermostatically controlled dry iron was introduced around 1937.

The calibration was changed to take in the main fabrics—linen (hot), cotton, wool, silk, rayon (cool). Since the late 1960s, on the recommendations of the HLCC, thermostats have been calibrated by code numbers which correspond to the 'care' labels found in garments and on textiles, though on some irons a fabric guide is printed alongside each setting.

STEAM-OR-DRY IRON

In 1953, Hoover launched the steam-or-dry iron. This is a two-in-one iron, giving a dry ironing for damp clothes, and at a touch of a switch producing jets of steam to dampen dry garments for pressing, or ironing. The average steam-or-dry iron rarely weighs more than 4 lb.

1967 saw the introduction of a spray steam-or-dry iron. This iron can spray a fine mist of water onto the material being ironed as well as being used for steam-or-dry ironing. This model is useful when extra dampening down is required. A sophisticated spray steam-or-dry iron will probably contain such conveniences as button slots, finger tip control for the temperature setting dial, an interchange right-hand, left-hand flex, and a water gauge.

NON-STICK SOLEPLATES

The end of the 1960s saw the arrival of the non-stick soleplate which is particularly useful for ironing starched fabrics. It is also stainproof and easy to clean.

PRESSES AND MANGLES

Household linen until the 17th or 18th century was pressed in heavy wooden presses. They were in various sizes to accommodate sheets and tablecloths, with a smaller type for table napkins.

The press consisted of two heavy, smooth wooden blocks set on a sturdy frame. The upper block could be raised or lowered by means of a turn-screw to release or increase the pressure on the linen which was laid smoothed and folded on the lower block.

MANGLES

Mangles must not be confused with wringers. Mangles were used for pressing and giving a shine to household linens; while wringers remove surplus water from wet clothes.

The mangle consisted of two large wooden rollers, set on a base, turned by a handle. It was possible to vary the pressure exerted by the rollers.

In a book on housekeeping in the mid-18th century the laundrymaid is instructed that mangling cloths should hardly ever be washed because with long, constant use they acquired a 'shining polish' which gave the linen a good finish. These cloths were of pale brown Holland, specially made for the job.

BOX MANGLES

Box mangles were enormous contraptions consisting of a large box filled with stones. This box was moved by a handle backwards and forwards over rollers. When the box reached the end of the pressing surface it could be tipped up. This allowed the rollers to be removed and the house-

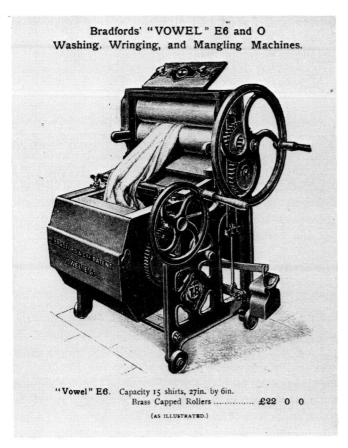

Bradfords' "VOWEL" E6 and O
Washing, Wringing, and Mangling Machines.

"Vowel" E6. Capacity 15 shirts, 27in. by 6in.
Brass Capped Rollers £22 0 0
(AS ILLUSTRATED.)

Washing, wringing and mangling
machine, 19th century. By permission
of the University of Reading
(Museum of English Rural Life).

hold linen to be placed on the pressing surface. The rollers were then
placed on top of the linen, the box set horizontal and the handle turned
thus setting the whole contraption in motion again.

Box mangles were for pressing household linen and were often found in
communal mangle houses and were shared by the women of the village.

It was a common sight in and around Cambridge in the 19th century to see a notice 'mangling done here' in a cottage window. The price ranged from 1d. to 4d. (½p to 2p, approximately) per basket.

ROTARY IRONERS

The modern equivalent of the mangle for pressing household linen and dry flat work is the rotary ironer, first introduced in Britain in the 1950s, although rotary irons had appeared in America in 1926. Rotary ironers have an electrically driven padded roller which revolves against a heated metal ironing shoe. The linen is pressed as it is carried between the roller and the ironing shoe. The heat of the shoe is thermostatically controlled. In some models the roller can be stopped and the heated shoe left switched on, so the ironer can be used as a press for trousers, skirts and dresses.

SOAP

It is impracticable to discuss the development of laundry equipment without including a brief mention of soap.

Soap, as a detergent or cleaning agent, has been in use for thousands of years. A Sumerian tablet from about 2500 BC contains a recipe for one part of oil to five and a half parts of potash to be used for washing cloth.

The Romans made a hard soap from goat's fat and wood ash boiled together. The soft potash mixture was then hardened by treating it with salt.

SOAP IN BRITAIN

A soap factory is thought to have been set up in Bristol as early as the 12th century. And Robert of Gloucester's Chronicle of the 12th century reports 'At Hartford sheep and axe (oxen) and fruit at Worcester, soap about Coventry, and iron at Gloucester.'

Boiling houses for making soft soaps were established in London and Bristol during the reign of Elizabeth I. The soap is reputed to have been made from fish oil and causticised wood ash. It must have been very harsh and smelt rather fishy! No wonder people were reluctant to bath. They can't have smelt any sweeter after a bath than they did before. Maybe the rich used a more luxurious soap made with olive oil, and imported from Castile in Spain.

Although soap was being made in Marseilles, Venice and Castile in some quantity, the industry was slow to develop commercially in this country. Materials were expensive and the industry strictly controlled. Charles I saw it as an additional source of revenue. He sold a charter to a group of London men who called themselves 'the London Society of Soap Boilers'. From this time soapmaking was restricted to areas within one mile of the centres of London, Bradford, and Bristol. The price of soap was controlled and a tax levied. More restrictions were imposed in 1710 when the British government curtailed any change in production methods.

SALT AS ALKALI

In 1793 a Frenchman, Leblanc, discovered that alkali for soap-making could be obtained from salt. This was soda. So now soap-makers no longer needed to rely on wood ash as a major ingredient. In the early 1800s, another Frenchman, Chevreul, showed how vegetable oils could be used instead of expensive animal fats. He also demonstrated that soap-making involved more than just mixing the ingredients into the correct consistency; but that chemical reactions took place when the mixture was boiled, which split up the fats into their fatty acids and glycerol constituents.

REPEAL OF SOAP TAX

The repeal of the soap tax by Gladstone in the mid-19th century after a cholera epidemic; the dirt, grime and grease of the industrial revolution; and the fashion in clothes which began to change with the development of the cotton industry, as cotton clothes were more easily washed than silks and satins, all helped to bring about the rapid development of the industry in the 19th century. Soap consumption rose from around 47,768 tons a year in England to 100,000 tons in 1861 and 260,000 tons by 1891.

The country people no doubt continued to make their own cleansing material from wood ash and animal tallow or fat. This mixture was generally known as a 'lye'. There were many different recipes for making lye, which might have contained such ingredients as wood ash, hen dung, pigeon dung. The bleaching properties of urine were also utilised—hardly hygienic.

W. H. Lever did much to increase the sale of soap by introducing branded and wrapped soap, and by launching an effective advertising campaign in the 1900s.

SOAP POWDER

In 1863 a crude soap powder was produced. This was a mixture of ground soap and alkalis; probably an adaptation of the housewife's own mixture of shredded soap and soda.

The next logical development was the introduction of different soaps for different jobs. Toilet soap, crude soap flakes and powders began to appear on the market. Lux flakes were first manufactured in 1900. This cutting up or chipping of the soap helped to increase the surface areas and solubility.

Persil was launched in 1909 and is reputed to be the first branded soap powder on the market.

NEW MATERIALS

In the early 20th century there was a shortage of animal fats, so manufacturers had to search for new raw materials. Olive oil had been used in soap making on the continent for centuries, but it was expensive and tended to make a soft soap.

German manufacturers discovered a method of hardening oils by hydrogenation. In this process oils are combined with hydrogen in the presence of a catalyst such as nickel or palladium. This process allowed the soap-maker to take advantage of a wider range of vegetable oils.

'Teflon' coating on iron sole plate prevents sticking of starch and fluff.

*Scrambled eggs, sticky sauces
and similar foods leave
almost no residue in a
saucepan with non-stick
finish. A dip in hot, sudsy
water and a wipe with a cloth
or soft pad removes all
grease. To be avoided: steel
wool and abrasive powders.*

A versatile collection of Teflon-finished cookware. The saucepan on the left incorporates an automatic stirrer. By permission of Tower Housewares.

SYNTHETIC DETERGENTS

Soap, particularly in hard water areas, is not the most efficient cleansing agent, and a major step forward in the evolution of the washday was the discovery of synthetic detergents. Synthetic detergents get their cleansing properties from their molecular structure which reduces the water tension and gives greater 'wetting' power. They function well in hard water as they don't react like soap with calcium and magnesium to produce a scum.

Research into the development of synthetic detergents was going on in France during the 19th century.

The first commercially viable synthetic detergent was produced in 1916 and called Nekal A. This early product reduced the surface tension, but it was not very good at removing dirt. Its main function was in the textile industry for washing wool.

The development of the oil industry in 1932 brought about the production of a synthetic detergent made from a mineral source rather than a vegetable or animal one. This was a sodium secondary alkyl sulphate. It was an excellent wetting agent, good at removing dirt, and had the advantage of not producing a lime scum in hard water.

SHORTAGE OF OILS AND FATS

The shortage of oils and fats brought about by the Second World War created the need to find other methods of producing an efficient detergent. 1942 saw the large-scale production of a liquid synthetic detergent, Teepol, and in 1944 the first synthetic detergent made from coal gas was introduced under the name of Lissapol N.

These detergents were satisfactory for light-duty washing such as woollens and crockery. More research was needed to produce the synthetic detergent powders we know today, which are suitable for heavy duty washing such as white work (i.e. sheets, pillowcases etc), as well as for light duty washing.

In the 1950s detergents manufactured from a petroleum derivative established themselves as an efficient alternative to soap and soap powders.

SOFT DETERGENTS

The main advantages of soapless detergents over soap is that they lather more efficiently in hard water. They brought, however, the problem of foam on rivers and sewage plants. A recent development has been the production of a simpler structured detergent which can be more easily broken down. These are known as biodegradable or 'soft' detergents, and all British products on the home market are now of this type.

BIOLOGICAL DETERGENTS

These contain enzymes which are added to normal detergent ingredients. The enzymes react on and help remove protein stains.

Enzymes are complex organic molecules produced by living cells, but they are not alive themselves. Examples of enzymic reactions can be seen in bread and cheese making, and in fermenting wine and beer.

Their use in removing protein stains, such as egg and blood, is not new. A patent for their use in this way was taken out in Germany in 1913. 'Spotting' preparations used for the removal of protein stains by dry cleaners and commercial launderers make use of enzymes.

The first enzyme product was sold in Britain in 1965 and was intended only as a prewash soak. In 1968 a washing powder combining detergents and enzymes was introduced, although these had been used for domestic washing as early as 1936 in Switzerland and Germany.

FURTHER READING

Washing Machines—Yesterday and Today. G. A. Williams. Electrical Times, April 10, 1958.

A Launderer's Chap-book. Published by Procter & Gamble Ltd.

Detergents. Elaine Moore, M. A. (Oxon). A Unilever Educational Booklet. Revised Ordinary Series no. 1, 1967.

Washday (R)*evolution*. Sheena Brooke. *Home Economics*, March 1970.

An Age of Machines 1871–1966. Moonbeams. Published for the employees of Procter & Gamble Ltd, June 1966.

Household and Country Craft. Allan Jobson. Elek Books Ltd, 1953.

The English Housewife in the 17th Century. Christina Hole. Chatto & Windus, 1953.

Housekeeping in the 18th Century. Rosamond Bayne-Powell. John Murray, 1956.

Ironing Today and Yesterday. Rosemary McRobert. Forbes Publications Ltd, 1970.

Washing Wisdom. A Guide to Modern Home Laundry. K. J. Mills. Forbes Publications Ltd, 1969.

Simple Laundrywork and Fabric Care. I. M. Mennie. Mills & Boon Ltd., 1972.

8 The Kitchen

The use of time has been a great force in the evolution of the kitchen. Our ancestors were not bound by the clock as we are today, and they had plenty of pairs of hands and feet to fetch and carry stores to and from dark cellars, barns, and ice-houses in the garden.

Kitchen scene, Italian, 17th century. Engraving after a picture by Antonio Tempesta. By permission of the Radio Times Hulton Picture Library.

Cottage interior with old woman preparing tea, 1793.

A vivid and apt description, which can apply to most homes up to the early 20th century, is given by Walter Buehr in *Home Sweet Home in the Nineteenth Century*: 'Every house was a long-term storehouse and large scale processing plant that required constant labour round the clock.'

THE TRANSITION

The 1914–18 war began the transition in housekeeping, as women were required for jobs outside the home which had been the prerogative of men. This caused a chronic labour shortage, particularly of domestic workers. So the gradual evolution of the kitchen from a large dark room below stairs with an unwieldy kitchen range to a bright modern room, with some consideration for time and motion study, which could be run by a housewife rather than a battery of servants, was under way.

*A farmhouse kitchen, early 19th
century. By permission of the Radio
Times Hulton Picture Library.*

The great momentum towards labour-saving devices, planned storage,
preparation and cooking facilities, and the use of colour in the kitchen
stems from the fact that, for the first time, the middle-class housewife had
to do her own cooking and housework, and was seen to do it by her
husband. Working conditions that had always been thought good
enough for servants were then rapidly found to be intolerable. By a
combination of education, personal influence and purchasing power, the
new style housewife demanded and got the improvements that we know
today.

A labourer's house at Whitmarsh, Warwickshire, Illustrated London News *April 13, 1872. By permission of the Radio Times Hulton Picture Library.*

THE KITCHEN UNIT

By the 19th century kitchen equipment was being produced on a limited scale by specialist manufacturers. Custom-built dressers and kitchen cupboards were part of the kitchen scene, though dark cellars, sculleries and pantries were still much in evidence.

Kitchen fittings during this period were being varnished and wooden floors covered with linoleum to make for easier cleaning.

The kitchen of the 1920s and 1930s was a confusion of unrelated design and finishes, containing little more than a sink with a draining board, a kitchen cabinet or old-fashioned dresser, a free-standing table, and some form of cooking and water heating appliance.

The housewife soon began to realise that she had only one pair of hands and feet to be her willing servants, and that she needed her stores and kitchen equipment easily to hand, not tucked away in some deep, dark cupboard or larder.

The kitchen cabinet, mentioned below, was in fact the storage revolution of the 1920s and could be considered the first piece of multi-purpose kitchen furniture. It superseded the ancient kitchen dresser.

American in origin, the kitchen cabinet was introduced into this country by a Canadian, Wilson Crowe, in the early 1920s. It consisted of a working surface, usually of vitreous enamel, in the form of a fall front, with storage space above and below, and cutlery drawers. In some designs the lower drawers were lined with tin to accommodate bread and flour.

It was a flexible unit in that it was free-standing and could be moved around to suit the particular situation. It also managed to cope with a surprising number of storage problems, though the main food storage space continued to be the larder.

CO-ORDINATION

F. B. Gilbreth, the American efficiency expert, started the revolution in co-ordination in the time and motion study related to housework. By the late 1930s a co-ordinated kitchen concept was accepted in America, and manufacturers were prepared to look at and think of a kitchen as a whole entity rather than as a collection of unrelated bits and pieces. Some architects were realising the efficiency and convenience of continuous working surfaces.

STANDARDISED UNITS

The 1939–45 war brought about the BSI standardisation of sink units and storage units to allow for the mass production of basic utility furniture, which was the only household furniture produced during the war.

After the war the kitchen cabinet was still popular, although a system of modular storage furniture, designed to a standard unit, was shown at the Britain Can Make It Exhibition in 1946.

It was the withdrawal of government restrictions on building in the 1950s which allowed the public to start considering the luxurious practicalities of the home, such as a comfortable, efficient and easy to clean kitchen, with 'at hand' storage space.

WORK SEQUENCE

The Council of Scientific Management in the Home (Co-Smith) produced a report *Meals in Modern Homes* during the early 1950s, which set out in detail what was entailed in preparing meals in the kitchen. This report was the first of its kind in this country. On the basis of this survey Co-Smith designed a kitchen which demonstrated a logical work sequence of work-top—sink—work-top—cooker—work-top at the Ideal Home Exhibition in the early 1950s.

This work sequence was further developed to storage—preparation—sink —cooker—serving and was established as the logical basis of kitchen planning. It began to be incorporated into new homes and kitchen conversions and is still used today.

Every family has different requirements but the sequence of work in the kitchen remains basically the same. The layout can be galley shaped, U-shaped, L-shaped provided the sequence remains logical.

OFF-THE-PEG UNITS

In the early 1950s kitchen units, which could be bought off the peg and allowed for individual tastes and requirements, and which could be added to as the occasion arose, were making an appearance on the market.

By the end of the 1950s this unit system had considerably evolved and now contained food store units with interior wire racks and adjustable shelving. There were also built-in arrangements for appliances, as well as wall units with built-in lights and spice storage fitments.

This basic unit continues to evolve as more research is undertaken into kitchen planning and the philosophy of storage.

FUTURE STORAGE SPACE

In a survey *Food Storage Facilities in Centrally Heated Flats*, the Council of Scientific Management in the Home suggested the following way of achieving adequate and efficient storage space:

i. a refrigerator unit with compartments at different temperatures;
ii. a ventilated food storage unit with insulated wall and double door;
iii. a tall unit, including a mid-height built-in refrigerator, and lower insulated compartment drawing air under the plinth from outside.

So perhaps by the end of the century, kitchen units will contain temperature storage units with different degrees of ventilation and thermal conditions which will cope with all types of food preservation, from deep frozen foods to tins, in a single combination.

SURFACES AND COLOUR

The high fashion for colour in the kitchen before, during and immediately after the Second World War, tended to be green and cream with a dark line, usually black, separating the colours.

The housewife, depressed and bored with the grey austerity of the war, and now spending more and more time in her kitchen, began to look for and demand more congenial working conditions, particularly a cheerful and attractive decor.

The development of plastics for domestic use brought about a significant transformation in kitchen design, in that it offered easily maintained surfaces and colour. It was now possible to eliminate dark corners by the use of light colours in the form of paint, tiles, or laminated plastics sheeting on the walls.

One of the first strong colours to be introduced into the kitchen, some eighteen years ago, was Formica's plastic laminate in Scarlet Red Softglow. It was used as a worktop on English Rose kitchen units which were made of pressed steel.

Colour pigments in the early 1950s were expensive and, consequently, paints were only available in pastel colours. So early colour schemes for 'modern' kitchens were pastel coloured paint on the walls and strong colour for the plastic laminated worktops, such as red, yellow and sky blue.

As the cost of pigments became cheaper, manufacturers of kitchen units began to consider colour for the vertical surfaces, such as cupboard doors and drawer fronts. This and the development of polyester finishes and thinner laminates, which provided a hardwearing finish to vertical surfaces, brought colour into the kitchen with a bang. Today there are colours and patterns to suit all tastes.

TOMORROW AND TOMORROW

The art of housekeeping which caters for the main essentials of life—food, shelter, warmth and comfort—has come a long way in the last five hundred years. It has developed as man's scientific ingenuity has evolved, until we have today's technical age.

What of the future? Will it become more and more stereotyped with less and less choice? A package deal for all except the wealthy who will afford to buy the exceptional? Of kitchens, a well-known consultant has said that by the end of the next decade we shall undoubtedly be able to produce the Package Deal Kitchen that can be bought on a single bill, installed by one team and maintained by one firm on a single annual service charge.

But will we need kitchens? According to Magnus Pyke's latest book *Technological Eating*, food will be the exception and pills and powders will be the rule. But man needs a craft in this day of mechanical giants. Take away the craft of creating a home and a garden, and he will perhaps lose his soul—the heart of his home.

FURTHER READING

Kitchens—planning notes. Council of Industrial Design.

The Kitchen. Joan E. Walley. Constable & Co.

Space in the Home. Ministry of Housing and Local Government. HMSO, 1963.

Kitchens. John Prizeman. (A Design centre Publication.) Macdonald & Co. Ltd, 1966.

Home for Today and Tomorrow. Ministry of Housing and Local Government. HMSO, 1961.

The Evolution of Food Storage. Sheena Brooke. *Home Economics*, May 1970.

Housework and Human Kinetics. Sheena Brooke. *Home Economics*, October, 1967.

Recommendations for Provision of Space for Domestic Kitchen Equipment, BS 3705. HMSO.

Kitchen Planning. Marjorie Campbell. *Home Economics*, January 1969.

Appendix
Looking and Collecting

Museums can be overwhelming places. There is so much to see that you can easily become confused and obtain a rather muddled picture of rural life in early days.

Before you visit a museum decide which part of the past interests you, say, mechanical ironing equipment from the 19th century onwards. If possible, do a little research beforehand to get an idea of what you are looking for.

It you like drawing take a sketching pad as this will help you to remember detail, otherwise make notes. It is impossible to remember all the information you will see.

Some museums have postcards of various exhibits and others publish quite comprehensively illustrated guide-books.

When you get home compare what you have seen with the equipment you use today. What are the main differences? Would *you* like to go back to, say, the 19th century and cope with the laundry of that period with the appliances available?

Pictures can tell you a lot about different periods. They may not tell you much about laundry equipment of the time but they will show you the type of clothes which needed ironing and pressing with the tools available. You will probably gather from this that fashion and ironing go hand in hand—one has been made necessary by the other; and that equipment has developed because of changes in fabric and fashion, and of course because of man's mechanical ingenuity. There are also many kitchen scenes with pots, pans, spits and so on.

All these little points help to build up a picture of the period you are interested in. They help it to come to life.

Some artists who have specialised in painting and caricaturing our domestic history are:

1. Thomas Rowlandson, 1756–1827, humorous drawings of everyday events.
2. William Hogarth, 1697–1764, a satirist of day-to-day life.
3. R. Seymour, 1800–1836, drew cartoons.
4. David Allan, 1744–96, has been called 'the Scotch Hogarth'.
5. David Wilkie, 1785–1841, was interested in interiors of the cottages, farms and houses of simple folk.

Some useful illustrations can be seen in:

An Encyclopaedia of Cottage, Farm and Villa Architecture and Furniture by J. C. Loudon, 1833. It has good illustrations of various cottages with sizes of rooms; it also contains illustrations and descriptions of solid fuel stoves, ovens and other domestic paraphernalia.

Illustrated English Social History. G. M. Trevelyan, O.M. Longmans, 1964. Is a good source of visual happenings.

So is *Life in Regency England*. R. J. White. B. T. Batsford, 1963.

The Great Exhibition, London 1851. Reprinted by David & Charles Ltd, 1970. This book doesn't contain many illustrations of domestic equipment but it gives an idea of the ornateness of Victorian times.

A detailed guide of museums and what they contain with hours of opening, *Museums and Galleries in Great Britain and Ireland*, is published by ABC Travel Guides Ltd, Oldhill, London Road, Dunstable, LU6 3EB, Bedfordshire.

THE LURE OF COLLECTING

More and more people are making small personal collections of domestic bygones. It is an interesting way of finding out about how our ancestors lived, and can make a visit to a town or village rewarding and exciting.

It can take the seeker into the past, showing her how other people lived and how this may have affected our lives today. It can also open the door to a whole host of new friends.

Most collectors are discriminating in that they specialise in a period or a particular subject. This narrows the field and makes the hunt more exciting, enabling the collector to become an 'expert'. The search for, say, salt spoons in various materials and designs can set in train a whole new approach to life.

It doesn't have to be expensive. Some of the most entrancing pieces have been picked up for a few new pence. There is something very satisfying in hunting down your own particular choice at market junk stalls, or the smaller antique shop which tends to display a collection of miscellaneous bits and pieces. This is the lure of collecting, persevering until you find exactly what *you* want.

Before setting out on the hunt it is quite a good plan to have a look at various collections. For instance, a Folk Museum will give you an idea of the range of domestic bygones.

READING

Our domestic history is not just the development of equipment and tools through the ages, it is involved with life—socially and politically, for instance the levying of the glass tax which brought about the engraving and cutting of glass.

The atmosphere of life is not easy to capture. We have to do more than look at and read about the utensils used by our forebears. To complete the picture we need to know about how people lived, how they worked and how they played, what were their problems and what were their joys. This is the background detail which gives our social history light and shade, shape and form.

This ambiance can be built up through reading novels, memoirs, diaries, biographies about the various periods in our history.

Advertisements in old magazines, papers and catalogues can give you an idea of the cost of living, as well as the different types of appliances available. A good hunting ground for old magazines and papers is provided by second hand-book stalls and shops. Some libraries keep back numbers. Two old catalogues have been reprinted recently; one of the Army and Navy Stores and the other of the Country Gentleman's Association 1894.

The following is a short list of books which may help to start you off:

The Diary of a Country Parson, the Rev. James Woodforde, edited by J. Beresford. Gives a vivid picture of life in the country during the 18th century.

Consuming Passions, A History of English Food and Appetite. Philippa Pullar.

The Englishman's Food by Sir J. C. Drummond and A. Wilbraham is a history of five centuries of food, diet and social change in England.

Food and Society by Magnus Pyke provides scientific and social information in a very readable form.

A History of Shopping by Dorothy Davis.

Edwardian England, 1901–1914, edited by Simon Nowell-Smith, includes an illuminating chapter by Marghanita Laski which gives a vivid description of what was expected of a domestic servant at that period.

Cranford, Elizabeth Gaskell. Deals with country customs and life during the early 19th century.

Novels by Jane Austen deal with the late 18th and early 19th century; those by Dickens, Thackeray, Trollope and Surtees with the middle and late 19th century.

Below Stairs, Margaret Powell. Gives an 'inside' view of a servant's life in Britain in the early part of this century.

Boswell's *Life of Dr Samuel Johnson* tells us something about life and social gatherings in the mid-18th century (especially in London).

John Galsworthy wrote about middle-class England during the later part of the 19th century to the mid-20th century.

Thomas Hardy wrote about life in the west country from the mid-19th to early 20th century.

Somerset Maugham and Agatha Christie are among many good sources of socially observant comment between the two World Wars.

The Stars Look Down. A. J. Cronin writes about Durham and Northumberland.

Brother to the Ox. Fred Kitchen writes about a farm labourer's life in Yorkshire at the turn of the century.

Index